Be Still
Quiet Moments with God in My Garden

Reflections on God's Steadfast Love

Patsy Kuipers

Foreword by Susan Hunt

Copyright © 2020 Patsy Kuipers

All rights reserved.

Scripture quotations are from The Holy Bible, English Standard Version® (ESV®), copyright © 2001 by Crossway, a publishing ministry of Good News Publishers. Used by permission. All rights reserved.

Although many publishers do not capitalize terms, particularly pronouns, which refer to the Trinity, the author has chosen to do so.

Portions of this book have been taken from the author's writings on her blog, www.patsykuipers.com, and revised and adapted for this format.

Cover Design: Josh Langston

Front Cover Photo: Patsy Kuipers

Back Cover Photo: Bruce Hornbuckle

ISBN: 978-1-7353733-3-1

"A beautiful and comforting book, Be Still is full of life-giving truths. As I read each devotional, I imagined walking with Patsy in Ray's garden, soothed by the splendor of unique plants while soaking up the depth and wisdom of life-changing treasures discovered through years of playing in the dirt and discovering beauty. Read Be Still slowly and allow Patsy to remind you to see the extraordinary in the ordinary and the majestic in the mundane."

-- **Sharon W. Betters**, Director of Resource Development, MARKINC Ministries.

"I wish you had the opportunity to sit at Patsy's kitchen table, overlooking her garden, and listen to her tell stories as she weaves in truths from God's Word, as she does in Be Still. Not just for gardeners, this book encourages readers to look for evidence of God's love all around them and helps them find hope and comfort in His Word, whether they're grieving specific losses or simply dealing with life's day-to-day challenges."

-- **Kathy Wargo**, PCA Committee on Discipleship Ministries Event Coordinator, Assistant to Women's Ministry Coordinator, Karen Hodge.

"It has been my distinct pleasure to work with and learn from Patsy, whose work is not only heartfelt and well-written, it's inspirational. I recommend it to anyone seeking solace in an ever more difficult time."

-- **Josh Langston**, bestselling novelist, editor, and writing instructor.

Dedication

To Mom, my life-long cheerleader and prayer warrior, with love and gratitude for your unwavering support.

And to Ray, the wind beneath my wings and my forever love.

Contents

Foreword *(Psalm 46:10)*
Author's Note *(Matthew 11:28-29)*
Prologue *(James 1:2-3)*

Glimpses of Glory *(Psalm 19:1-4)*

Garden Stories *(Genesis 2:8-9, 15)* **3**
Enlightened Eyes *(Ephesians 1:16-18)* **7**
A Nestful of Hope *(James 1:17)* **11**
He Didn't Have to Do It *(Genesis 1:11-12)* **14**
A Little Bit of Heaven (2 Corinthians 2:14) **17**
Pollen Season *(Genesis 8:22)* **20**
Let's All Sing *(Psalm 118:24)* **24**

The Benevolent Gardener *(Psalm 100)*

Sustainer of All *(Psalm 145:14-16)* **31**
Warmed by the Son *(2 Corinthians 1:3-4)* **34**
Feed the Birds *(Exodus 16:4-5, 17-20)* **38**
His Eye Is on the Sparrow (*Luke 12:6-7)* **41**
Streams of Water *(John 4:13-14)* **45**
Twiners and Climbers *(John 10:27-29)* **49**
What About the Little Things? *(Psalm 8:1, 3-5)* **53**
I See You! *(Psalm 139:7-12)* **56**

Planted Together *(1Peter 3:8-9)*

Passalongs *(2 Corinthians 5:19-20)* **61**

Are You Contagious? *(Psalm 141:3)* **64**

Bearing All Things *(1 Corinthians 13:7-8)* **67**

Mine! *(Job 41:11)* **70**

The Way the World Works *(Romans 8:22-23)* **74**

Letting Go *(Isaiah 43:18-19)* **78**

Cultivating Holiness *(Colossians 2:6-7)*

Ask *(James 1:5-6)* **83**

Superfood for the Soul *(Matthew 4:4)* **87**

Where's Your Focus? *(Luke 10:41-42)* **90**

Thrashing About *(Matthew 14:25-32)* **93**

The Imposter *(John 8:44)* **96**

Don't Tempt Me! *(1 Corinthians 10:12)* **99**

Weeds *(Matthew 13:3-4, 7)* **102**

Transformation *(Romans 8:28-30)*

Soul Amendments *(Ezekiel 36:26-27)* **109**

Prudent Pruning *(John 15:1-2)* **113**

Bearing Fruit *(Luke 6:43-45)* **116**

Exfoliation *(Ephesians 4:21-24)* **120**

Seasons *(Ecclesiastes 3:1-8)* **124**

A Tale of Three Trees *(Isaiah 61:1, 3)* **128**

When We Least Expect It *(2 Peter 3:9-10, 13)* **132**

Acknowledgements **137**

Foreword

Be still, and know that I am God.
Psalm 46:10

Patsy has been my friend, spiritual daughter, and part of the same local church for 28 years. I have watched her learn to be still when she

> arrived at our church and knew she needed a spiritual mother
>
> suddenly became a widow at age thirty-eight
>
> juggled motherhood and her professional life
>
> depended on her parents to help with childcare
>
> gave her daughters in marriage
>
> was unemployed when her job was eliminated
>
> returned to school to get a horticulture diploma
>
> became a grandmother
>
> began developing her gift of writing
>
> began caring for her parents as they age
>
> became a Bible study teacher, spiritual mother to younger women, and coordinator of the women's ministry in our church

Patsy has learned to be still because she knows He is God.

Her knowledge of the Triune One courses through her whole being and finds expression in her writing. And now she invites us to enter the stillness and to know the Savior better.

Susan Hunt

Former PCA Coordinator for Women's Ministry

Author's Note

Come to me, all who labor and are heavy laden, and I will give you rest. Take my yoke upon you, and learn from me, for I am gentle and lowly in heart, and you will find rest for your souls.
Matthew 11:28-29

Scattered. A word I often use to describe my thoughts, my activities, and my days. Numerous distractions and responsibilities vie for attention. They scramble my mind and weary my soul. But there's a place I can turn to for solace, a place where I spend some of my sweetest times with the Lord – my garden. There I'm reminded of the first garden and the promise of a new, redeemed garden. I see Jesus' parables come to life as I observe the flowers and birds, the seasons and soils. My spirit soars as I behold God's tremendous power, yet is quieted by the assurance that the One who cares for all creation also cares for me.

Several years ago, the lessons I've learned in my garden met up with my love of writing, and I began a blog, Back 2 the Garden (patsykuipers.com). I longed to share what God had been teaching me and to tell others of His great love and faithfulness.

As my portfolio of stories grew, so did the dream to compile them into a book, something that will be around for my children and grandchildren even after my blog and I are not. Five years in the making, *Be Still* is the fulfillment of that dream.

I've arranged the 35 devotional readings in *Be Still* in five categories, with distinct yet intertwined themes:

- ❖ Glimpses of Glory – evidence of God's love all around us
- ❖ The Benevolent Gardener – God's protection and provision
- ❖ Planted Together – principles for life-giving relationships
- ❖ Cultivating Holiness – disciplines of spiritual growth
- ❖ Transformation – God's work of sanctification

Each entry begins with a passage from the Bible and ends with a brief prayer. In between, you'll find the timeless truths of Scripture wrapped in simple stories. I pray they will encourage you to slow down and open your eyes to the wonders all around us, to be still and draw near to God.

Patsy Kuipers

Fall, 2020

Prologue

Count it all joy, my brothers, when you meet trials of various kinds, for you know that the testing of your faith produces steadfastness.
James 1:2-3

February 1998. Ten months earlier, my beloved husband, Ray, died of a heart attack a few weeks after his 39th birthday. Even though I was a rational person who could recount the details surrounding his death, I maintained a protective mantle of denial. How could my engaging, energetic mate go to work one sunny spring Saturday and never return home to our two young daughters and me? The reality dripped into my soul bit by bit and oozed through the cracks in my shield. The underlying pool of sadness crept over its banks and flooded many of my days.

Joy? Not so much.

In preparing for Ray's funeral, I wrote a letter for one of the pastors to read during the service. Among other things, I stated he'd not only left a lasting legacy in the lives of our daughters but also in the beauty of our garden. Ray had a horticulture degree, and though he didn't shun common plants, he preferred unique specimens for our yard. He told me about the diverse plants he had selected and patiently taught me their names. I helped weed, water, and mow but left landscape planning to him.

Several of Ray's horticulture colleagues paid a visit and walked the property with me after he died. Listening to them exclaim over first one plant and then another confirmed, yet again, that the garden was an exceptional part of his legacy.

It became equally evident I needed to learn how to take care of it; otherwise, it would merely be a matter of time before weeds overtook everything, much like sorrow entwined my thoughts.

And so that February day found me outside, bundled against the late-winter chill. I stooped to pull back the blanket of leaves shrouding the planting beds, my heart as numb as my fingers. I longed for Ray to be there, kneeling beside me shoulder-to-shoulder, to remove those leaves. Occasional tears watered the patch of soil where I labored.

I placed one handful of leaves after another into the big brown yard debris bag. Wait! What's that? I detected flecks of green amidst the weathered leaf litter. Perennials Ray had planted were beginning to emerge from the soil. Seeing those tiny-but-determined plants sparked hope within me. If they could make it through the cold, stark winter, maybe I would survive my season of darkness.

I didn't know it then, but I experienced my first session of garden therapy that day. And I caught a glimpse of the joy that comes from persevering, one of many lessons the Lord had prepared for me in His outdoor classroom

Glimpses of Glory

The heavens declare the glory of God,
and the sky above proclaims his handiwork.
Day to day pours out speech,
and night to night reveals knowledge.
There is no speech, nor are there words,
whose voice is not heard.
Their voice goes out through all the earth,
and their words to the end of the world.
Psalm 19:1-4

Garden Stories

And the LORD God planted a garden in Eden, in the east, and there he put the man whom he had formed. And out of the ground the LORD God made to spring up every tree that is pleasant to the sight and good for food . . . The LORD God took the man and put him in the garden of Eden to work it and keep it.
Genesis 2:8-9, 15

In My Genes

Sometimes I muse that gardening is in my genes.

To use one of Mom's old expressions, I suppose I come by it honestly. My grandfathers supported their families by farming in central North Carolina. My grandmothers canned, preserved, or froze the excess fruits of their husbands' labors, those not consumed or shared right after harvesting.

Memories of summertime Sunday dinners around their tables are vibrant even though decades have passed since I last sat elbow-to-elbow with relatives spanning several generations: plates of juicy red tomato slices and steaming corn on the cob; bowls full of fried okra, green beans, and lima beans; freshly-made biscuits and gravy. Laughter seasoned the conversation as family stories mingled with good-natured ribbing.

Other recollections are equally vivid – flowers edging the fields; straw hats perched on hooks by the door, ready to be grasped on the way out to the garden; a metal dipper hung on a nail above the back-porch sink for a refreshing sip of water upon returning to the house.

My mom was one of eight siblings, my dad one of ten. They, along with most of my aunts and uncles, gardened. Their efforts ranged from plots to grow a few vegetables to a commercial tomato farm, from fruit trees to flower-filled beds surrounding suburban homes.

Multiple members of my generation love tending plants, as do a number of our children and grandchildren. Recognizing our shared passion, I smile when cousins post pictures of their gardens, sometimes with young offspring sampling produce fresh from the vine.

And me? I'm a member of the "Play in the Dirt Club," a frequent-shopper program at a local nursery. I adopted their phrase years ago to describe my gardening ventures. Weeding, mowing, mulching, planting – I love playing in the dirt! I don't have a spot sunny enough to grow veggies, so my gardening efforts are focused on tending plants of the decorative variety. The delight I feel in caring for my flowers and shrubs is enhanced by the connection to generations of loved ones and the communion I feel with God and His creation.

The First Garden

Maybe the notion that gardening is in my genes isn't so far-fetched, at least when you consider where God placed our very first ancestors – in the Garden of Eden, an idyllic place, where all sorts of plants thrived, and God strolled in the cool of the evening. He entrusted them with the responsibility of maintaining the garden and gave them all the plants as food, save one, the tree of the knowledge of good and evil (Genesis 2:8, 15-17).

One exception amidst unimaginable abundance, yet Adam and Eve didn't obey. Satan cunningly twisted God's command and Eve ate, believing his lie that God was withholding something pleasant and necessary. She offered Adam a bite, and he ate. In a moment, everything changed (Genesis 3:1-7).

But God came to the garden, as always, even though He knew of their disobedience, and He drew them out of their hiding place. In the midst of declaring the penalties they'd incur, including loss of intimate communion with Him, God planted a kernel of hope, a promise they could count on. One day the Seed of the woman would bruise the head of the serpent, dealing death itself a fatal blow (Genesis 3:8-19).

Centuries passed, and the time came for God to send His beloved Son, that whoever believes in Him would not perish, but have everlasting life (John 3:16). Jesus left His place at the Father's right hand and dwelt among us for a while. On the night of His betrayal, He retreated with His disciples to the Garden of Gethsemane. With sorrow weighing heavily on His soul, He fervently prayed that the cup might pass from Him, yet He remained perfectly obedient to His Father's will, even to the point of death on the cross.

There was a new tomb in the garden near the place of Jesus' crucifixion (John 19:41). Joseph of Arimathea placed His body in that tomb, but death couldn't hold Him there. On the third day, God raised Him by the power of the Spirit. His atoning sacrifice made it possible once again for us to enter God's presence unafraid, to savor communion with our Maker.

The Redeemed Garden

So many significant garden events in His-story, with more to come. Jesus promised to return. When He does, heaven and earth will pass away, making way for the new heaven and new earth where God will dwell with His people forever (Revelation 21:1-4). God will redeem Creation right along with His children. And there will be a garden, watered by the stream flowing from the throne of God, where the tree of life will flourish.

One continuous story from beginning to end. Could it be the sweet connections woven through generations of gardeners in my family are rooted in echoes of Eden? Our hearts harbor a deep-seated longing for perfect communion with God in a world unmarred by sin. No more thistles and thorns. No more pain or tears or death.

O Lord, as we wait for Jesus' return, You gift us with hints of heaven – fruits and flowers and fresh-from-the-field vegetables, gatherings with friends and family around food-laden tables, and moments of communion with You while playing in the dirt. Let us give thanks, remembering even the most splendid day here is a mere shadow of the beauty that awaits in the redeemed garden.

Enlightened Eyes

I do not cease to give thanks for you, remembering you in my prayers, that the God of our Lord Jesus Christ, the Father of glory, may give you the Spirit of wisdom and of revelation in the knowledge of him, having the eyes of your hearts enlightened.
Ephesians 1:16-18

Camouflaged

I had opened my Bible study lesson but hadn't silenced my phone yet. It dinged three times in rapid succession, alerting me to incoming text messages, most likely of the group variety.

My curiosity piqued, I had to look. After all, I hadn't officially settled into my quiet time. The glance confirmed my hunch. Daughter Jessie had sent a photo to her sister, Mary, and me, with the comment, "Fun game! Let me know when you spot it."

Mary replied without hesitation, "Cool!!!"

I stared at the up-close photo of a tree trunk, admiring the bark, but had to enlarge the image before I found the hidden critter and exclaimed, "That guy is super camouflaged!"

Jessie conceded, "I totally wouldn't have seen the moth except he was sitting right below a trail blaze (blue rectangles painted around the trail so you can keep track of it), and I had looked up at the blaze just by chance."

Our pleasant text conversation came to an end. I silenced my phone and turned my attention back to the lesson before me, astounded to read, "Unless a power beyond us opens our eyes, we will blindly walk right past the infinite magnificence of God's treasure. We take for granted the glorious truth in Christ: we are God's beloved children."[1]

Talk about an immediate spiritual application of Jessie's trail blaze experience!

Blessing Upon Blessing

The Apostle Paul, writing to the Ephesians, proclaims, "Blessed be the God and Father of our Lord Jesus Christ, who has blessed us in Christ with every spiritual blessing in the heavenly places" (Ephesians 1:3).

Paul then goes on to recount those blessings. In Christ, we are

- ❖ chosen by God before the foundation of the world, that we should be holy and blameless before Him (v. 4)
- ❖ predestined for adoption to Himself (v. 5)
- ❖ redeemed (v. 7)
- ❖ forgiven (v. 7)

---

[1] Lisa Tarplee,"Hinged, Vitally Connected to Christ and His Church, Women's Bible Study on Ephesians," Week 2, CDM Discipleship Ministries, 2020, p. 31.

- ❖ made recipients of the riches of God's lavish grace (vv. 7-8)
- ❖ given wisdom and insight to understand God's plan of redemption (vv. 9-10)
- ❖ made heirs (vv. 11-12)
- ❖ sealed with the promised Holy Spirit, the guarantee of our inheritance (vv. 13-14)

Next, Paul prays for the eyes of our hearts to be enlightened that we may know

- ❖ the hope to which God has called us (v. 18)
- ❖ the riches of God's glorious inheritance in the saints (v. 18)
- ❖ the immeasurable greatness of His power toward those who believe – the same power that raised Jesus from the dead (v. 19)

Fueled by that kind of power, you'd think we'd be better at living out the reality of all the blessings heaped upon us, confident and unafraid because of our status as beloved children of the King. But too often, our spiritual sight is clouded by immediate demands, our ears filled with voices clamoring for our attention. The temporal hides the eternal as effectively as the moth's disguise allowed it to blend into the bark.

Seeing and Hearing

Jesus frequently taught in parables, many of which had a connection to plants – sowing, reaping, seasons, soils. When his disciples asked why He spoke in parables, He replied,

> "To you, it has been given to know the secrets of the kingdom of heaven, but to them it has not been given... Indeed, in their case the prophecy of Isaiah is fulfilled that says: 'You will indeed hear

but never understand, and you will indeed see but never perceive.' . . . But blessed are your eyes, for they see, and your ears, for they hear." (Matthew 13:11, 14, 16)

Blessed indeed! Jesus came not just to restore sight and hearing to those physically blind and deaf, but to open our spiritual eyes and ears to His message and the evidence of His love all around us. And when Jesus ascended to heaven, He didn't leave us as orphans. The Father sent the promised Helper to be our trail blaze (John 14:16-17, 26).

Even so, we must be intentional about seeing and hearing.

Interludes spent in my garden allow me to be still in God's presence, to look and listen deliberately. Time after time, Jesus' parables come to life as I tend the plot of land God has entrusted to me. I stroll my property searching for treasures I imagine God's tucked lovingly here and there for me to find. Years of practicing these purposeful walks have honed my sight, enabling me to recognize even barely-there plants as they emerge from the soil. How much more should I purposefully seek to know the things of God, to perceive the guidance of His Spirit, and to hear His still, quiet voice by becoming intimately acquainted with the treasures found in His Word?

O Lord, how I thank you for enlightening the eyes of our hearts to recognize the blessings You've lavished upon us. Please help us to be ever-attentive to the leading of your Spirit that we may see the path You've set before us with increasing clarity.

A Nestful of Hope

Every good gift and every perfect gift is from above, coming down from the Father of lights, with whom there is no variation or shadow due to change.
James 1:17

Helping Mama Bird

Having a seriously-ill wife was stressful enough for my dad. Then the painting company scheduled my parents' house for the week I transferred Mom from the hospital to a rehab facility. Any home improvement project comes with its attendant potential for tension, and this job was no different. The workmen arrived early and stayed late, accompanied by the sounds of clanging ladders, humming pressure washers, and pounding hammers.

Uh oh! As they prepared to clean the deck, they found a lovingly-crafted nest containing four tiny blue eggs. Under normal circumstances, the location selected by the mama bird – perched on a ladder stored horizontally under the deck – would have been ideal, out of sight of predators and protected from the elements. But these were not normal circumstances. Knowing the commotion of scouring and staining the deck would most likely scare the mother away and that the high-powered stream of water might damage the small home, the painters carefully moved the ladder out of their work zone.

However, the new resting place for the ladder left the nest and its not-yet-hatched tenants fully exposed. Would the mother abandon her brood? Would an enemy eat the eggs as they lay within easy reach? Oh, the anxiety! My dad became a second mother to the little ones, and each evening he gave me a report.

Once the painters had returned the ladder to its usual spot, with the nest still positioned on its metal perch, Dad checked on its occupants. Not only were all four eggs present, but the baby birds were also beginning to hatch. The next day, Dad resumed his vigil from inside. After seeing no sign of the mother bird, he headed outside to the little ones, a cup of water and an eyedropper in hand. Hydration duty complete, he debated what to feed them. Fortunately for him and the hatchlings, mama bird returned and faithfully cared for her babies in the ensuing days as they grew and eventually left the nest.

Divine Diversions

God was so good to give my dad something to take his mind off Mom's precarious condition, at least for brief respites during her time away from home. The week the baby bird saga was unfolding coincided with my annual observation of the anniversary of my husband's death. As I read through journal entries I had made shortly after his passing, I came across these words, penned the day after his burial: "Picked out a grass marker for Ray's grave, then went to (my aunt's) for lunch and to see the baby bunnies again. They're adorable, as are the baby chickadees she showed us. Lord, thank You for the reminder, amidst our sadness, that life goes on and that there are still blessings and beauty to be enjoyed."

This world is full of brokenness. From minor disappointments and broken promises to aging bodies, terminal illness, and death, proof abounds that things aren't the way they were in the beginning, the way God intended them to be. But evidence of His love and sustaining power is all around us – reminders that He hasn't left us and never will.

Fluffy white masses towering in a blue summer sky. Busy bees with full pollen baskets. Birds singing their praises to the One who assures us if He cares for the lilies and sparrows, He'll certainly care for His children (Matthew 6:25-34). Your list will look different, my friend, but make that list.

Look for glimpses of heaven. **Listen** for whispers of love from our Father who attends to every detail of our lives. **Taste and see**, the Lord is good; His love endures forever! (Psalm 34; 1 Chronicles 16:34; Psalm 106:1)[1]

Lord, Your gifts are all around us. Please help us to think about these things and to be grateful for the pure, excellent, lovely aspects of this life that point us to the life to come.

---

[1] These are just a few of the many, many verses that speak of the Lord's steadfast, enduring love. Use a concordance or Bible app and search for "steadfast love endures" sometime!

He Didn't Have To Do It

And God said, "Let the earth sprout vegetation, plants yielding seed, and fruit trees bearing fruit in which is their seed, each according to its kind, on the earth." And it was so. The earth brought forth vegetation, plants yielding seed according to their own kinds, and trees bearing fruit in which is their seed, each according to its kind. And God saw that it was good.
Genesis 1:11-12

God's Garden

The first time I visited The Pocket at Pigeon Mountain near LaFayette, Georgia, in search of spring ephemerals,[1] it was unseasonably cold. Snow flurries swirled through the crisp air while I huddled close to my fellow wildflower enthusiasts in an attempt to avoid the brunt of the biting wind. I don't even remember if anything was blooming.

The cold snap was short-lived, and two weeks later, I

---

[1] Ephemeral plants are generally found in deciduous woods. They take advantage of the sunlight available in early spring before the leaves return to the trees. They bloom and decline in a relatively short period of time, lasting from a few days (e.g. trout lilies) to a few weeks (e.g. trilliums) depending on the plant.

returned to find the gently sloping terrain adorned with such a vast array of wildflowers I could barely take it in. I asked my companion if someone had planted the astounding assortment. "No," he explained. "The soils and conditions here are such that it developed naturally."

From that moment on, I've thought of The Pocket as God's Garden, where the Creator's ingenuity is on magnificent display. To my believing heart, I recognized and embraced it as an incredible gift from a loving Father.

Exceeding Abundance

When I went back to school to study horticulture after completing a 30-year career with a large corporation, I was amazed at the number of different plants. For example, there are nearly 600 species of oak trees and 250 species of camellias. By comparison, I learned Latin and common names for a mere 300 plants in my woody and herbaceous ID classes. I soon realized I could happily study horticulture for the rest of my life without draining the well of knowledge.

My newfound awareness led me to contemplate the creative capacity of the One who spoke everything into existence. God could have fashioned one kind of tree, a solitary selection of shrub, a single type of rose, and left it at that. But He didn't! I wonder if the vast array of plants (not to mention people, animals, and insects) isn't a result of the sheer exuberance of creating coupled with God's desire to instill joy in us when we see His glory reflected in the complexity and splendor all around us.

To be sure, life in this world can be difficult. From personal hardships to international conflict, we don't have to look far to find trouble. But we don't have to look far to find evidence of God's abiding love either. My heart sings when I'm at The Pocket, but it also soars when I discover a returning perennial peeking out of the leaves in my woods, watch my grandchildren master new skills, or listen as a friend shares how God is working in her life.

Lavish Love

Before the foundation of the world, God knew the choices we'd make, how we'd turn away from Him. Still, He spoke this amazingly beautiful world into existence. He created men and women in His image and placed them in a perfect garden. Yet Adam and Eve tried to usurp His rightful place, something their progeny have desired to do ever since.

Complete in Himself and lacking nothing, God could have turned away from His ungrateful creatures. But He didn't! Instead, He sent His one and only Son to save us. Jesus was pierced for our transgressions; His punishment brought us peace; His wounds healed us (Isaiah 53:5). Therefore, we have the promise of abundant life now and eternal life in His presence when He returns to restore all things.

From the tiniest wildflower to the gift of eternal life, God overlooks no detail as He affectionately pours out boundless blessings upon His children.

O Lord, You didn't have to save us. Nothing in us merits Your steadfast love or Your compassion and kindness, much less the precious blood of Your Son. We praise and thank You for sending Jesus to redeem us and for surrounding us with ample evidence of Your goodness.

A Little Bit of Heaven

Thanks be to God, who in Christ always leads us in triumphal procession, and through us spreads the fragrance of the knowledge of him everywhere.
2 Corinthians 2:14

Heaven on Earth

The first whispers of spring beckon me to consult my calendar in anticipation of my annual pilgrimage to The Pocket. No matter how many times I visit this mecca for wildflower devotees, reverent awe accompanies me as I stroll. The site's beauty rivals that of any man-made cathedral. From the canopy of newly-birthed leaves to the gurgling brook and flower-bedecked slopes, God's handiwork is everywhere. Swaths of native plants line the path, their patchwork occasionally interrupted by massive, moss-covered tree trunks toppled long ago. Birds contribute their songs to the brook's background music.

The palette changes week by week during wildflower season as some species decline and others take center stage. I've yet to fulfill my desire to visit once a week for the four peak weeks of the season; nonetheless, doing so remains high on my wish list. In the meantime, I've designated a small section of my wooded backyard as a mini-Pocket.

It may sound presumptuous to try to imitate that heavenly haven on my property. Still, I'm gradually introducing some of the native plants found there – trilliums, wood poppies, Virginia bluebells, bloodroot, Solomon's plume. Though it's a shadow of the original, it allows me to experience the same sense of wonder each spring as the plants reawaken and take turns in the spotlight.

The Aroma of Christ

As I was contemplating my attempts to recreate some semblance of The Pocket, several lines from the Lord's Prayer came to mind: "Our Father in heaven, hallowed be your name. Your kingdom come, your will be done, on earth as it is in heaven" (Matthew 6:9-10).

We often think of this request in terms of Jesus' triumphant return, when He'll vanquish all God's enemies and establish His kingdom forever. However, Jesus proclaimed, "The time is fulfilled, and the kingdom of God is at hand; repent and believe in the gospel" (Mark 1:15). God's plan of salvation reached its climax when Jesus willingly went to the cross, bore our sins, suffered the punishment we deserved, and rose victoriously from the grave. His atoning death secured our eternal destiny.

For now, though, we're in this world, living in the now and not yet. We're alive in Christ and seated in the heavenly places (Ephesians 2:5-6), yet we struggle as sojourners in our earthly tents (2 Corinthians 5:1).

But we're not alone! When Jesus ascended back to the

Father, He sent the Holy Spirit to comfort and counsel us, and to conform us more and more to His image. We are to be salt and light, to bear witness to God's grace, ever-ready to give an answer for the hope within us. Jesus calls us to take up our cross and follow Him. We're to love others as He loves us.

Finite human beings looking like Jesus sounds as unlikely as my attempts to replicate The Pocket in my woods. But the transformative power of the Spirit accomplishes what would be impossible apart from Him. Furthermore, by embracing our identity in Christ and embodying His characteristics, we become His ambassadors to a watching world. Through us, God spreads the fragrance of the knowledge of Christ everywhere we go. How amazing!

Dear Lord, thank You for the power of Your Spirit at work within us. Please help us to bring a little bit of heaven into the lives of those who come our way, be it for a moment or a lifetime. May they see You in us as we represent Your kingdom on earth until You return.

Pollen Season

While the earth remains, seedtime and harvest, cold and heat,
summer and winter, day and night, shall not cease.
Genesis 8:22

The Yellow Invasion

I first noticed the yellow dusting atop my dark-blue Honda CR-V. Then it appeared on my black mailbox. Within days I found it sprinkled across everything from leaves to walkway to my work boots. What might the stealthy invader be? Pine pollen!

I usually grimace when I detect the initial signs of yellowness that descends on our area each spring, knowing what lies ahead. Depending on rainfall or lack thereof, the layer of pollen can become so thick tire tracks materialize on driveways and footprints on sidewalks. Some years I watch incredulously as windblown clouds drift off pines, destined to coat everything in their path, including people and pets. Nothing is immune from the intruder.

But in spring 2020, when most news reports included the descriptor "unprecedented," and we added phrases like "social distancing" to our vocabulary, the opening salvo from the annual interloper made me smile. It reminded me God was keeping the covenant promise He made to Noah, his offspring, and every living creature.

God's Regret

God had become so angry with the evil in men's hearts that He regretted ever creating them and sent the flood to wipe them out:

> The Lord saw that the wickedness of man was great in the earth, and that every intention of the thoughts of his heart was only evil continually. And the Lord was sorry that he had made man on the earth, and it grieved him to his heart. So the Lord said, "I will blot out man whom I have created from the face of the land, man and animals and creeping things and birds of the heavens, for I am sorry that I have made them." But Noah found favor in the eyes of the Lord. (Genesis 6:5-8)

How sad and sobering to think that men's wanton disobedience grieved the heart of God so much that He wanted to rid the earth of them. But He preserved a remnant for Himself through Noah and made a covenant sealed with a rainbow. God's promise, recorded in the introductory verse above, came as a welcome pledge after the devastating deluge.

We don't have to look far to find examples of evil intentions and behavior in our day. Even those of us who belong to God continue to wrestle with sin. When things like a pandemic, natural disasters, and social unrest mount up, we can't help but wonder if they are signs of God's displeasure and discipline. Or possibly even the beginning of the end (Matthew 24:3-8).

Promise Keeper

As the closures and restrictions associated with the coronavirus quickly accumulated, bringing a halt to the rhythm of daily life, the pollen came as a timely reminder of God's promise to Noah. Amidst the uncertainty and upheaval surrounding COVID-19, spring arrived, full of hope and visible proofs of God's character. He is merciful and gracious, slow to anger, and abounding in steadfast love and faithfulness (Exodus 34:6). He keeps His promises and is faithful even when we are not (2 Timothy 2:13).

2020 progressed, and troubling circumstances continued to pile up. I reminded myself repeatedly, sometimes multiple times a day, that there's more than this life to look forward to. In his letter to the Corinthians, Paul acknowledges that our outer selves are wasting away. Still, he says our afflictions are light and momentary when compared with the eternal weight of glory that awaits. He goes on to encourage us to "look not to the things that are seen but to the things that are unseen. For the things that are seen are transient, but the things that are unseen are eternal" (2 Corinthians 4:16-18).

One day, the world will come to an end. Jesus will return and gather His covenant people, the remnant preserved for Him across all of history. Until then, God will graciously sustain His creation and provide visible reminders, like rainbows and pine pollen, of unseen things. Assurance that we can trust Him to fulfill all of His promises.

Glimpses of Glory

O Lord, we endeavor to look to the unseen things that will never pass away, but how we appreciate the visible evidence of Your watchcare over us and all creation. You are a sure stronghold in times of trouble and never forsake those who put their trust in You.

Let's All Sing

This is the day the LORD has made; let us rejoice and be glad in it.
Psalm 118:24

New Every Day

If you've ever visited Disneyland, I bet the three-word title caused a colorful tropical image to pop into your head, accompanied by the rest of the stanza, " . . . like the birdies do, tweet, tweet, tweet, tweet, tweet."[1] You may even be humming the tune sung by the inhabitants of the Enchanted Tiki Room, where "the birds sing words and the flowers croon." [2]

The cheerful ditty came to mind repeatedly one summer because of a mockingbird who had taken up residence in my crape myrtle. The majestic tree's canopy reaches across much of the front of my house and above the roofline, shading my bedroom windows and provided a proper perch for the

---

[1] "Let's All Sing Like The Birdies Sing" was written in 1932 by a team of songwriters lead by English composer Tolchard Evans.
[2] Songwriters: Richard M. Sherman / Robert B. Sherman, "The Tiki, Tiki, Tiki Room" lyrics © Walt Disney Music Company.

mockingbird to serenade me. I often heard it singing soon after I awoke, prompting me to think, "That bird sounds so happy!" And then, "I can rejoice and be exceeding glad, too, because God has allowed me to wake up to another day."

But sometimes, I want to burrow under the covers instead, my enthusiasm stifled by the demands and uncertainties looming in the hours ahead. Even so, Scripture is full of assurances:

- ❖ God's mercies never fail. They are new every morning (Lamentations 3:21-23).
- ❖ Jesus acknowledged we'd have troubles in this world but went on to say, "Take heart. I've overcome the world" (John 16:33).
- ❖ If God cares for the birds who sing so sweetly, He'll surely take care of us, His beloved children (Matthew 10:29-31).

Musical Ties

During challenging times, these and other promises comfort me in the form of lyrics from beloved hymns. I'll start whistling the tune and then instantly transition to singing complete verses aloud. "Great is Thy Faithfulness," "It is Well with my Soul," "What a Friend We Have in Jesus," "Be Thou My Vision," and our family anthem, "Amazing Grace." Such is the power of music to encourage, enlighten, and connect.

Mom grew up attending a tiny Presbyterian church in the equally-tiny town of Gulf, North Carolina. Some eight decades later, when the first few strains of a hymn familiar since childhood emanate from the piano at our current church, she smiles, leans over, and whispers, "That's a Gulf song!" I nod and return her smile as we fondly recall the white wooden structure and the loved ones buried in its cemetery, links in our heritage of faith.

When my now-adult daughters were little, my husband Ray and I used "Amazing Grace" as a lullaby. Though their dad died when they were in elementary school, leaving them with few memories of their godly father, they clearly remember him singing them to sleep with that classic hymn.

When my grandchildren were born, I continued the tradition their grandfather and I began with their mother, soothing them to sleep with "Amazing Grace," planting seeds of faith from their earliest days. Six-year-old Lyla is prone to humming as she works on a craft project or tackles one of her small household chores. I believe it's an overflow of her happy heart. Occasionally she'll sigh, "I've got this song stuck in my head!"

Frequently the song on replay is a hymn. How wonderful to have God's Word sewn into our hearts with threads of music, binding us to Him and to generations of fellow believers as we follow nature's cues in singing His praises!

Let All Creation Sing

Hearing the shouts of adoration as Jesus rode triumphantly into Jerusalem, the Pharisees, indignant and no doubt jealous, said, "'Teacher, rebuke your disciples.' Jesus answered, 'I tell you, if these were silent, the very stones would cry out'" (Luke 19:39-40).

The psalmist shares similar sentiments, "The heavens declare the glory of God, and the sky above proclaims his handiwork. Day to day pours out speech, and night to night reveals knowledge. There is no speech, nor are there words, whose voice is not heard. Their voice goes out through all the earth, and their words to the end of the world" (Psalm 19:1-4).

Indeed creation does praise the Creator in myriad ways. Yet we who've been the recipients of God's great love and mercy are best equipped to articulate all He's done for us. So let us sing with joyful abandon like the mockingbird outside my window, proclaiming His goodness and faithfulness, as we rejoice in the gift of each new day.

Dear Lord, please help us to rejoice and be exceeding glad, even on days when responsibilities and concerns press in upon us, knowing Your grace is sufficient to meet all our needs.

The Benevolent Gardener

Make a joyful noise to the LORD, all the earth!
Serve the LORD with gladness!
Come into his presence with singing!
Know that the LORD, he is God!
It is he who made us, and we are his;
we are his people, and the sheep of his pasture.
Enter his gates with thanksgiving,
and his courts with praise!
Give thanks to him; bless his name!
For the LORD is good;
his steadfast love endures forever,
and his faithfulness to all generations.
Psalm 100

Sustainer of All

The Lord upholds all who are falling and raises up all who are bowed down. The eyes of all look to you, and you give them their food in due season. You open your hand; you satisfy the desire of every living thing.
Psalm 145:14-16

Winter Wonderland?

Despite the previous evening's forecast for "just a dusting," I awoke one December morning to a world already cloaked in white, as more fluffy flakes floated earthward. I made a harried trip to the grocery store and returned home before the roads became slippery. Safely nestled in my warm house with plenty of supplies, I settled in to witness the rare event unfolding outside. A line of near-freezing cold from the North made acquaintance with plenty of moisture from the South over our swath of Georgia, resulting in perfect conditions for an abundance of beautiful snow.

My initial delight gradually turned to concern as I beheld trees bending closer and closer to the ground, their branches succumbing to the weight of their heavy blanket. I love plants and do my best to care for the ones on my small suburban property. Thus, when the precipitation slowed to a halt mid-afternoon, I bundled up and ventured outside to free them from their frosty burden. Armed with an old broom, I began to gently poke, push, and sweep snow from trees and bushes. I was relieved to see limbs of azaleas and camellias, dogwoods and maples reach skyward once again. I labored for nearly an hour before retreating inside, satisfied I'd done what I could to help my plant friends, at least the ones within my reach.

And then the snow resumed. The flakes' persistent descent proceeded throughout the evening and into the night. I peered out my front windows, checking on trees that were once again drooping perilously. The serenity of the scene illuminated by the streetlight belied the danger posed by the mounting accumulation. I eventually gave up my vigil and crawled into bed, fearing my efforts earlier in the day may have been in vain.

Benevolent Rays

Precipitation had ceased by the time I made my way downstairs the following day, but the sky was steely. I hastened to measure the accumulation before it was disturbed by frolicking neighborhood children. Almost ten inches shrouded my yard, an amount unheard of since the Blizzard of '93. With a sinking heart, I made note that many of my trees and shrubs were still pitifully bent, and some bore broken branches.

The gray scene soon gave way to a glistening fairyland. Clouds dissipated, revealing a brilliant blue sky and sunshine that skipped across the sparkling mantle of white. As I watched, the benevolent rays and a gentle breeze began to free the trees from their frozen constraints, accomplishing much more than I could with my broom. Snow fell in slivers and chunks. Limbs commenced to thaw and unfurl.

Good Stewards

I smiled sheepishly, acknowledging that the Lord is fully capable of caring for His creation, that I am a steward and He is the owner. Every plant, bird, blade of grass are His. God doesn't need our help. Nevertheless, He not only allows and enables us to take part in caring for our world and each other, but He also commands us to do so (Genesis 1:28; James 2:15-16).

He has entrusted each of us with gifts and resources to use for His glory and has placed folks in our sphere of influence that we might minister to them in various ways. As members of the body of Christ, we each have a meaningful, God-ordained role to play (Romans 12:4-13; 1 Corinthians 12).

It's weighty enough to be good stewards of the material resources God has consigned to us, much less the well-being of the people who share our lives, especially our children and grandchildren. What if I mess it up? What if my best efforts fall short, like my attempts to clear the snow from my precious plants? Our peace and assurance come from remembering He is God, and we are not. He will surely accomplish His purposes in and through us and the ones we love.

Lord, please help us to have a proper view of our place and our efforts. May we be faithful stewards of that which you've entrusted to us, but let us never forget You are Sovereign over the outcome. Grant us your peace as we trust You in all things.

Warmed by the Son

Blessed be the God and Father of our Lord Jesus Christ, the Father of mercies and God of all comfort, who comforts us in all our affliction, so that we may be able to comfort those who are in any affliction, with the comfort with which we ourselves are comforted by God.
2 Corinthians 1: 3-4

Fall Planting

Summer heat often stretches into September here on the outskirts of Atlanta. But when it finally releases its grip, we're usually blessed with several weeks of more moderate weather, perfect for playing in the dirt. My husband Ray used to purchase perennials from the end-of-season clearance aisles, knowing the straggly specimens would flourish the next year once in the ground and given the proper care. Even though I would shake my head at the sight of his motley gaggle of pots containing soil but little visible foliage, I've adopted his practice.

You see, contrary to popular belief, fall, not spring, is the best time to plant most perennials. As air temperatures cool, top growth gradually comes to a halt. Since soil temperatures drop more slowly, the plant can then shift additional energy to its roots, thereby establishing a robust network to convey water and nutrients to support its next round of growth the following year.

I Killed It!

Several years ago, I had accumulated a multitude of pots reminiscent of Ray's. I'd purchased some of the plants and acquired others from the gardens of generous friends. Numerous commitments interfered with my garden activities that fall. By the time I had an opening on my calendar, an uncharacteristic chill had descended on our area. Not one to be deterred from my mission to get the plants out of their pots and into the ground, I proceeded to spend several hours happily planting my new friends. Even though I couldn't feel my toes and fingers, the day's work warmed my heart.

As forecast, temperatures that night dipped below freezing. When I got downstairs the next morning, I went to the kitchen window overlooking the woods and scanned the scene, trying to ascertain how the plants had fared in the frigid conditions. The native sweetshrub was upright, its bright yellow leaves a cheerful beacon in the early morning light. The Fatsia were slightly drooped, yet still green. But where was the beautiful 'Pink Frost' anise[1] that had enchanted me the day before with its spicy scent and lovely green leaves outlined with a margin of creamy white? Surely that brownish mass of sagging leaves wasn't it?!

I quickly pulled a heavy coat on over my PJs, slipped my feet into my work boots, and headed to the woods for a closer

---

[1] *Illicium floridanum* 'Pink Frost'.

look. Alas, it was the anise. Its leaves so graceful and aromatic the day before were stiff. At that moment, I think I knew what Charlie Brown must have felt like when he put the first ornament on his spindly little Christmas tree, only to watch it bend to the ground, overwhelmed by the weight. "I've killed it!" As I trudged back inside, I scolded myself with thoughts of "Why didn't I heed the forecast and leave the anise in its pot in a sheltered area?"

Despite a brisk wind and below-average temperature, the sun shone brightly throughout the day. Several hours after I had made my initial trek to the woods, I peered out the window again. Much to my surprise, the color had returned to the anise! Once more, I made my way to the woods for a closer look. The lovely leaves were supple and fragrant. Like Charlie Brown's tree, all it needed was a bit of love and care. In this case, the TLC came from the sun's radiant beams.

The Son's Warmth

There are times when chilling winds blow through our lives. They present themselves in myriad forms and cover the spectrum from harsh words to the loss of a loved one. I've embraced Elisabeth Elliot's all-encompassing definition of suffering: "Suffering is having what you don't want or wanting what you don't have."[1]

Jesus told us to expect tribulations in this world, but He also spoke words of peace, encouraging us to take heart because He had overcome all the hardships we'd face (John 16:33). He is the Light of the World, guiding and reassuring us along the way. The warmth of His presence, which radiates to us through His

---

[1] Elisabeth Elliot, *Suffering Is Never for Nothing* (Nashville, B&H Publishing Group, 2019), p. 9.

Word and the loving concern of others, revives and restores our weary souls. And each time it does, it strengthens our faith, enabling us to store up the essentials we'll need to grow again.

Furthermore, God instructs us not to keep His comforting warmth to ourselves but to provide that same compassionate care to others who've been pried from their familiar pots and planted in trying territory. As His comfort flows through us, may it rekindle their hope, warm their chilly hearts, and prepare them to flourish anew.

Father, please help us to love others well because You have loved us so well, to care for them as You care for us, and to shine Your light of hope for all to see.

Feed the Birds

Then the Lord said to Moses, "Behold, I am about to rain bread from heaven for you, and the people shall go out and gather a day's portion every day, that I may test them, whether they will walk in my law or not. On the sixth day, when they prepare what they bring in, it will be twice as much as they gather daily." . . . And the people of Israel did so. They gathered, some more, some less. But when they measured it with an omer, whoever gathered much had nothing left over, and whoever gathered little had no lack. Each of them gathered as much as he could eat. And Moses said to them, "Let no one leave any of it over till the morning." But they did not listen to Moses. Some left part of it till the morning, and it bred worms and stank. And Moses was angry with them.
Exodus 16:4-5; 17-20

Morning Ritual

Within a few days of my placing the first birdfeeder on a sturdy hook attached to my deck, the birds became accustomed to dining on the seeds it held. Now, several years and multiple iterations of feeders later, they continue to rely on me to fill and refill their food supply. As their dependence on me grew, so did a corresponding sense of responsibility on my part. I now consider them to be my outdoor pets!

But sometimes, especially in the summertime when the sun and birds rise earlier than I do, I descend the stairs to my kitchen and find some of my friends already waiting for breakfast.[1] They hop along the railing and perch on the hooks as if to say, "Hey! Remember us?!"

It may be my imagination, but there are times I've been scolded by chickadees when I'm tardy returning the feeders to their hangers. The clipped chirps of these black-capped cuties convey, "Finally! What took you so long?"

And then there's the fun of hearing birds signaling each other from various locations in the woods. I like to think they're calling back and forth, "Breakfast is ready!"

My efforts are rewarded by the return of hungry guests almost before I get back inside. I delight in the relationship that's developed between these small creatures and me. In caring for them, I know I'm helping keep an eye on some of God's sparrows. I wonder if He takes joy in watching me partake of all He provides just as I relish watching the birds feast on the seeds and suet.

Never Late

Unlike me, though, God is never late in supplying what we need. The scripture passage above recounts how God

---

[1] I have to bring the feeders in at night because they also attract raccoons and opossums!

provided manna for His hangry people who were complaining against Moses and Aaron for bringing them into the wilderness to die. They even went so far as to say they would have been better off in Egypt, where they had had plenty of meat and bread (Exodus 16:1-3). Then God miraculously bestowed bread from heaven, and there were still some who didn't trust Him enough to follow His instructions regarding the extraordinary provisions.

It's easy for us to read these accounts and think, "What's wrong with these people?!"

They saw the plagues. They watched Moses part the Red Sea. They witnessed the Egyptian soldiers' demise as the waters rushed over them after the Israelites had crossed on dry land. And yet they doubted God's ability to provide for them and questioned His goodness, thinking they'd be better off as slaves of Pharaoh than children of the true King.

Learning to Trust

Then again, are we so different? Despite experiencing the Lord's provision across six decades of life, when faced with trying circumstances I am still prone to think, "Uh oh. What am I going to do now?"

But those years of savoring God's tender oversight have taught me to wait expectantly, like the birds who flock to my woods each morning. I can say with the psalmist, "I have been young, and now am old, yet I have not seen the righteous forsaken or his children begging for bread" (Psalm 37:25).

Lord, You are a good, good Father, providing all we need. Please help us to trust Your timing and Your sufficiency. And may we ever praise and thank You for your loving care.

His Eye Is on the Sparrow

Are not five sparrows sold for two pennies? And not one of them is forgotten before God. Why, even the hairs of your head are all numbered. Fear not; you are of more value than many sparrows.
Luke 12:6-7

Storm Warning

Unlike tornados that pop up with little advance notice, potential hurricanes can be tracked by meteorologists from the time they're born as tropical waves off the coast of Africa. Scientists watch, name, and categorize them. They model their paths, and when conditions merit it, they issue warnings so people can prepare before their arrival.

Such was the case in September 2017. As Hurricane Irma plowed her way through the Caribbean, it became evident her interaction with the tiny islands wouldn't slow her down. Not only was Irma expected to wreak havoc in Florida, but she was also big enough and strong enough to trigger a tropical storm warning for metro Atlanta, where I reside.

I checked the forecast frequently over the weekend,

fretfully wondering when we'd feel the brunt of the storm. Finally, the models zeroed in on late Monday afternoon. I spent Sunday evening bringing potted plants into the garage, securing outdoor furniture, and pondering how many of the trees might still be standing on Tuesday. Even though I trust God to work all things together for good, I couldn't completely rid myself of an undercurrent of anxiety. I went to sleep, praying for protection for all in the storm's path.

Unfazed Feeders

I awoke Monday, still praying, something I would continue throughout the day. A gentle rain pattered on the roof. An occasional breeze-nudged branch tapped the house. And then I heard them. My bird friends had arrived for breakfast, as usual. A glance at the weather forecast – no high winds predicted until later in the day – gave me the confidence to hang the larger of the two feeders for a few hours. I had barely closed the door to the deck before my feathered companions flocked to their meal. Soon I perceived the characteristic call of the red-bellied woodpecker prompting me to return the suet, his favorite treat, to its hanger.

Rain fell throughout the day, steady showers repeatedly giving way to relentless downpours, as Irma's blustery remains coursed through our area. Despite the challenging conditions, birds continued to flit from branch to feeder to tree trunk, seemingly oblivious to the circumstances.

I repeatedly returned to the bay window that overlooks my woods, hoping to somehow will the trees to keep standing with my frequent and fervent gazes. All the while, I petitioned the One with the power to keep them upright to protect me, my neighbors, and our property. As I watched the green canopy sway in the increasing gusts and beheld the unperturbed behavior of the birds, calm pervaded my spirit. The scene before me embodied one of Jesus' most precious lessons: our Father, who cares for the birds of the air and the lilies of the field, will surely care for his children. Those who trust in Him need not worry about tomorrow (Matthew 6:25-34).

Our Refuge

Many of the storms in our lives aren't meteorological. They have nothing to do with barometric pressure or wind speed. Broken relationships, health issues, the death of a loved one – these and other tempests enter our lives, often unexpectedly. Yet nothing ever catches God by surprise, and we can count on His promise never to leave or forsake us, regardless of the source of the upheaval (Deuteronomy 31:8).

Even so, there are times we see only the storm, forgetting the One who commands the wind and rain. We're in good company. Jesus' disciples feared for their lives when a fierce windstorm descended on the lake they were crossing. Jesus was asleep in the boat, but the waves swamped their vessel and their vision. Jesus scolded them for their lack of faith, but He didn't hesitate to calm the storm-tossed lake (Matthew 8:24-26).

The Lord deals with us in much the same way, remembering we are dust, frail creatures who sometimes lose sight of Him amidst our storms. As our compassionate Father, He sends reassurances of His watchful care. On the day Irma blew through, my reminder came via the unruffled presence of the birds as they visited the feeder, trusting and unafraid.

I strolled my property the following day, picking up a few

downed branches, praising God that there was no significant damage. And then I saw it – a tiny cyclamen nestled at the base of a towering oak, protected from the storm. What a picture of the refuge we have in the Lord Almighty!

Lord, thank You for your patience and compassion when we're afraid. Please help us to rest in the assurance that if You watch over the tiniest of Your creatures, You'll certainly watch over Your children.

Streams of Water

Everyone who drinks of this water will be thirsty again, but whoever drinks of the water that I will give him will never be thirsty again. The water that I will give him will become in him a spring of water welling up to eternal life.
John 4:13-14

Watering Well

Water is essential for all life forms, and watering plants correctly is critically important to their health. When we moved to Georgia, we noticed many of our neighbors installed automatic sprinklers. We opted not to do so, but that didn't keep my late husband, Ray, from commenting (to me, not our neighbors) regarding others' use of their systems.

Though Ray was an easy-going type, he would sometimes become miffed when he saw gardening faux pas. Watering is an area rife with misconceptions and missteps. More is not necessarily better, and over-watering can drown a plant, killing it as fast or faster than not watering it enough.

Likewise, repeated, shallow watering can do more harm

than good. Though newly-planted specimens require frequent watering during their initial establishment phase, continued daily spritzes, like those we saw with the irrigation systems that ran for a few minutes every day, can lead to plants having weak, shallow roots. The plants grow accustomed to the practice and have no incentive to dig deeper into the soil for sustenance.

In contrast, when you water plants deeply and less often, they develop more robust roots, ones that grow in search of sources of water lying further beneath the soil. The plants can then withstand times of drought. And they don't topple over easily since they're firmly anchored in the ground.

Well-Watered

Ray's sound watering principles remind me of several Bible passages that liken the righteous to well-watered trees. With their roots sunk deep into the rich soil of God's Word, they're able to flourish, even when faced with harsh conditions:

- ❖ Psalm 1:1-3 describes how the righteous don't walk or stand, much less sit with the wicked. They don't linger to take sips from polluted waters of disbelief but saturate themselves in the life-giving words of the Lord by meditating on them day and night. Thus, like trees planted by streams of water, they prosper and bear fruit.
- ❖ Psalm 92:12-15 says the righteous will continue to bear fruit into old age, like vibrant trees, full of sap and evergreen. Their mission? To declare that the Lord is

upright. As Isaiah proclaims, they are oaks of righteousness planted for God's glory (Isaiah 61:3).
- ❖ In Jeremiah 17:7-8, God declares that those who trust in Him are secure. Like trees with their roots extended to a nearby source of water, they are not anxious because God Himself will preserve them.

Living Water

The concept of life-giving water runs like a stream through the pages of scripture. When the Israelites grumbled against Moses for leading them into a desert where they had nothing to drink, Moses cried out to God for help. The Lord provided water from a rock (Exodus 17:5-6). Commenting on this episode in his letter to the Corinthians, the Apostle Paul leaves no doubt that the Rock was Christ (1 Corinthians 10:4).

Indeed, Jesus referred to Himself as the Source of Living Water when He spoke the words recorded in the introductory verse above to the Samaritan woman who came to draw water from the well.[1] Later, Jesus made a similar proclamation, "If anyone thirsts, let him come to me and drink. Whoever believes in me, as the Scripture has said, 'Out of his heart will flow rivers of living water'" (John 7:37-38). What a remarkable promise for those who believe – the indwelling Spirit will produce living water in us in such abundance that it will not only benefit us but will also refresh others.

---

[1] You can read the full account of Jesus' encounter with the Samaritan woman in John 4:1-30.

And the living water isn't just for this life. Take a look at the description of the new Jerusalem in Revelation:

> Then the angel showed me the river of the water of life, bright as crystal, flowing from the throne of God and of the Lamb through the middle of the street of the city; also, on either side of the river, the tree of life with its twelve kinds of fruit, yielding its fruit each month. The leaves of the tree were for the healing of the nations. (Revelation 22:1-2)[1]

Unlike the shallow showers from our neighbors' sprinklers, the life-giving water flows abundantly in the heart of believers, sustaining us now and through all eternity!

O Lord, what a blessing to have streams of living water flowing through us by the power of the Spirit. Please help us to drink deeply of your life-giving Word that our faith roots may become more vigorous, enabling us to flourish and bear much fruit for Your glory.

---

[1] Take time to read a parallel prophecy in Ezekiel 47:1-12 for a beautiful description of the sufficiency of the water flowing from the temple in the new Jerusalem.

Twiners and Climbers

My sheep hear my voice, and I know them, and they follow me. I give them eternal life, and they will never perish, and no one will snatch them out of my hand. My Father, who has given them to me, is greater than all, and no one is able to snatch them out of the Father's hand.
John 10:27-29

In simplest terms, vines are plants whose stems require support unless they're left to trail along the ground. They use various methods to climb and attach themselves to supporting structures, including twining stems, tendrils, aerial roots, and adhesive disks, also known as holdfasts.[1] Observing their behavior has led me to some spiritual comparisons.

Tenacious Tendrils

Tendrils are plant organs specialized to anchor and support vining stems, distinctive because they possess a powerful twining tendency, encircling any object encountered. They're sensitive to contact and will turn toward objects they brush against.[2] Think curly-cue fishing line – slender but sturdy.

---

[1] https://web.extension.illinois.edu/vines/attachment.cfm

During a customary reconnaissance stroll through my woods, I discovered a patch of passionflower vine that had popped up. The baby vine was already sprouting tendrils and reaching out for support. I smiled and shook my head when I found one tiny green appendage wrapped around a fallen oak leaf. Even though the tendril had a stranglehold on the leaf, the latter could never help the passionflower rise above the ground.

Tendrils borne on another sprig of vine clutched a more promising but still less-than-ideal platform, a squat neighboring plant. I fetched a trellis from the garage and returned to the woods, determined to pry the tendril free from the leaf and unwrap those twirled around the unsuspecting coral bells. As I guided them to the trellis, nudging the tendrils to grasp the appropriate support, I thought how prone we are to engage in misguided attachments.

Created in the image of the Triune God, we're relational beings, designed for community. But we often look to fellow finite sojourners to meet needs only God Himself can fill, overwhelming or alienating them in the process.

Or worse, we turn to things to fortify us. Though God commands us to worship Him and Him alone, we tend to worship created things instead of the Creator. At times, our hearts are like tendrils that turn toward whatever they brush against.

Praise God for sending the Spirit. Like a sturdy trellis, He is our Helper and Counselor, our all-sufficient, strong-enough Support (John 14:26).

---

[2] https://www.britannica.com/science/tendril

The Benevolent Gardener

Clinging Climbers

Virginia creeper can scale walls and tree trunks thanks to holdfasts that act like sticky toes. Though capable of ascending considerable heights, it's easy to dislodge.

I once yanked a Virginia creeper off the side of my daughter's house. Nourished by plentiful rainfall, it had clambered up to the roof and put down roots in the gutter. Nonetheless, a few tugs brought the entire vine tumbling down as its little feet let go of the wall. Unlike the wayward tendrils in the first story, the vine picked a solid underpinning. But when faced with the adversity brought about by my tugging, it didn't have the strength to hold on.

In 1997, the year my husband Ray died, Christian artist Geoff Moore released his album *Threads*, which concluded with "The Letter." The lyrics tell of someone ready to give up but encouraged not to do so by the friend who received his letter. As I struggled to regain my footing after Ray's sudden death, these words brought hope and comfort:

> And when your hand starts to slip
> And when you're losing your grip
> And when you know your hope is gone
> You're not the only one holding on.[1]

There were many times I had to remind myself God was holding me and would never let go.

More recently, I learned the hymn, "He Will Hold Me Fast," whose lyrics offer the same assurance found in the Geoff Moore song:

---

[1] "The Letter" © 1997, The ForeFront Communications Group, Inc. Lyrics by Geoff Moore. Music by Geoff Moore and Joel McCreight.

Be Still

> When I fear my faith will fail,
> Christ will hold me fast;
> When the tempter would prevail,
> He will hold me fast.
> I could never keep my hold
> through life's fearful path;
> For my love is often cold;
> He must hold me fast.[1]

Jesus' declaration, recorded in the introductory verses from the Gospel of John above, underlies the assurance found in these songs. We're secure in the Father's hand, where no one will be able to snatch us away.

Dear Lord, how we thank You for sending Your Spirit to be our ever-steady Support. We praise You for the precious promise that though our strength may fail, You'll never let us go. We're forever safe in Your mighty grasp.

---

[1] Ada R. Habershon, "He Will Hold Me Fast," 1906.

What About the Little Things?

O Lord, our Lord, how majestic is your name in all the earth! You have set your glory above the heavens. . . . When I look at your heavens, the work of your fingers, the moon and the stars, which you have set in place, what is man that you are mindful of him, and the son of man that you care for him? Yet you have made him a little lower than the heavenly beings and crowned him with glory and honor.
Psalm 8:1, 3-5

If you're like me, you expect God to take care of the big things. You know, making sure the sun rises and sets, keeping the ocean in bounds and the stars in their places. After all, He's the omnipotent, omniscient, omnipresent One, with no beginning and no end.

My heart rejoices like that of the psalmist over God's might and magnificence. I can also relate to the rest of his proclamation. It's often the quiet moments and tiny details that leave me speechless, for it's then He reminds me that He knows me intimately.

Be Still

Beyond My Control

Even though my property is relatively small, I've left much of it natural and have incorporated numerous unique and native plants into my landscape. Unlike more traditional suburban lawns that require mowing and edging, caring for my garden involves careful handwork. It takes an abundance of patience to gently pull weeds so as not to uproot desirable plants nestled close by, unwrap vines cinched tightly around azalea branches, and selectively prune shrubs instead of shearing them into geometric shapes.

Because of the time-intensive nature of maintaining my landscape, weeds and vines sometimes threaten to take over. Such was the case several years ago when well-meaning friends offered to assist. My dismay over my yard's appearance overrode concerns about the varying levels of my helpers' horticultural knowledge. I tried to match people to tasks and supervised the various work areas as my friends labored diligently on their assignments.

However, there was too much going on for me to keep track of everyone. Despite my friends' good intentions, they damaged a few of my plants. A post-work-session inspection revealed no sign of my trillium, a cherished wildflower salvaged years before during a plant rescue. One of the guys used a leaf blower to clear some of the flower beds, not realizing my spring ephemerals, including the trillium, were too fragile to be subjected to the gale-force winds produced by the blower. I was heartbroken, knowing I would have to wait until the following year to see if it would reemerge.

Heavenly Father

To my relief, the trillium survived the trauma and returned the next spring, even bigger and more beautiful than

The Benevolent Gardener

before. But that's not all! Imagine my surprise and delight two years later when not only did the mama trillium reappear, but several babies also came up in the woods. I consulted one of my horticulture mentors. The most logical explanation for the appearance of those new trilliums, located many feet from the mother plant? The seeds were dispersed unknowingly by the fellow brandishing the leaf blower! God took something I thought was a loss and turned it into a gift, a cause for joy and celebration.

I know Almighty God will handle the big things. He spoke the world into existence, raised Jesus from the dead, and holds everything together. Yet this all-powerful God sees me, loves me, and repeatedly stoops to bless me with small, ideally-suited gestures. Each time He does so, I'm humbled and amazed that Almighty God is also Abba, Father.

So it is for each of His children. He sees us as individuals, uniquely knit together with different combinations of strengths and weaknesses, hopes and fears, yet each bearing His image. He predestined us for adoption through Jesus (Ephesians 1:5). He redeemed us and calls us by name (Isaiah 43:1). Let us never forget that we belong to a loving Father, the ultimate gift-giver who is sovereign over every detail.

O Lord, thank You for adopting us. As Your beloved children, we have the privilege of addressing You as Jesus did, "Abba! Father!" We gratefully marvel at Your patient, personal care.

I See You!

Where shall I go from your Spirit? Or where shall I flee from your presence? If I ascend to heaven, you are there! If I make my bed in Sheol, you are there! If I take the wings of the morning and dwell in the uttermost parts of the sea, even there your hand shall lead me, and your right hand shall hold me. If I say, "Surely the darkness shall cover me, and the light about me be night," even the darkness is not dark to you; the night is bright as the day, for darkness is as light with you.
Psalm 139:7-12

A Timely Greeting

Do you ever have weeks where troublesome events pile up, leading you to wonder what might happen next? The end of such a week several years ago found me hunkered down emotionally, bracing for the next volley. Even so, I was cautiously optimistic when Saturday of the exceptionally trying week dawned, reminding myself the Lord's mercies never fail, that they're new every morning (Lamentations 3:21-24).

I was barely halfway down the stairs, looking forward to a day at home to do a few chores, maybe some writing and a little

The Benevolent Gardener

weeding, when I saw it. Instead of facing outward toward the sun like its fellow flowers, one beautiful blossom on the Rose of Sharon[1] on my front porch was peeking in the left sidelight. A joyful, irrepressible exclamation escaped my lips, "Good morning, Lord! Thank You!!" I knew, without a doubt, Who was responsible for the perfectly-placed greeting.

Encouraging Onlooker

Several years ago, my kids introduced me to *American Ninja Warrior*. The amazing athletic feats performed by the participants plus their inspiring backstories combine to make the show an anticipated staple of my summer TV lineup. Often, as a contestant makes his or her way through the obstacles, drawing closer to the podium where the announcers stand, one of the hosts will yell encouragingly, "I see you (insert name of ninja)!"

The Lord's Saturday morning salutation shouted, "I see you, Patsy!" It was a reminder that none of what had transpired the previous week went unnoticed by the One who's promised never to leave me or forsake me. The image of that flower stayed with me throughout the day and still makes me smile because my loving Father had reached out in such an intimate way. I don't think it's far-fetched to imagine Him smiling as well, watching as His delighted daughter gazed out the window, appreciatively acknowledging His floral gesture, which found its mark like an impeccably-aimed arrow.

Comforting Watchfulness

Some may find the idea of never being out of God's sight unsettling. After all, none of our actions, honorable or

---

[1] *Hibiscus syriacus*

dishonorable, escape His view. I agree that it is a formidable thought, yet it serves to restrain my behavior. Like a grateful child, I want to please my kind, compassionate Father.

Moreover, I find comfort in knowing God always sees me. Years ago, before cell phones equipped with GPS and Find My Friends, I'd be on some dark country road in one of the Carolinas, returning from a customer call, thinking, "No one in the whole world knows where I am right now. But God does."

It is equally comforting to know God's watchfulness extends to our children. There are countless moments across a lifetime when parents whisper a prayer and wonder what will happen when their children are out of their sight. When we drop them off at kindergarten or watch them back out of the driveway for the first time with their sibling in the passenger seat, or help them move into their college dorm and leave them miles from home. How reassuring to know they won't be out of God's sight for even an instant no matter where they are. He'll always see them. And us (Psalm 34:15).

O Lord, what a blessing it is to know Your eyes are ever upon us and those we love, how precious when You send us personal reminders of Your watchfulness.

Planted Together

Finally, all of you, have unity of mind, sympathy, brotherly love, a tender heart, and a humble mind. Do not repay evil for evil or reviling for reviling, but on the contrary, bless, for to this you were called, that you may obtain a blessing.
1 Peter 3:8-9

Passalongs

In Christ God was reconciling the world to himself, not counting their trespasses against them, and entrusting to us the message of reconciliation. Therefore, we are ambassadors for Christ, God making his appeal through us. We implore you on behalf of Christ, be reconciled to God.
2 Corinthians 5:19-20

Sharing Our Plants

Sharing plants is one of the many joys of being a gardener. The tradition is particularly strong in the South. In fact, some varieties known as passalong plants aren't readily available for purchase. Instead, they've survived for decades by being passed along from one generation of horticulture enthusiasts to the next.

I'm blessed to have numerous plants given to me by fellow plant lovers: hosta from an aunt who had the greenest of thumbs; a hydrangea grown from a cutting of a friend's father's plant; multiple trilliums dotting the woods, offspring of a lone rescue plant. There are also mayapples, spurred violets, and several varieties of ferns. The list would be quite extensive if I cataloged each leafy gift. And then there are all the treasured items my husband Ray planted that continue to flourish over 20 years after his passing.

Tending these plants, anticipating their return each year, and watching them grow gives me a great deal of pleasure. The pleasure is multiplied by remembering the people and circumstances which led to them being in my garden. I also think of plants I've shared now growing in friends' gardens, and I smile at the connections they create.

Sharing Our Faith

As much as I relish exchanging plants, I recognize I've been entrusted with something much more precious to pass along: my faith. Although trusting God and acknowledging Jesus as Savior and Lord are gifts only God can give, He commissions us to tell others about His great love (Matthew 28:19). Our first responsibility is to our families. God commands us to teach our children His decrees, integrating our lessons into all of life – when we sit in our house, when we walk by the way, when we lie down, and when we rise (Deuteronomy 6:6-7).

But our mandate to reach others with the good news doesn't end there. We are to be light, living in such a way that we glorify our Father, always prepared to explain the reason for our hope (Matthew 5:14-16; 1 Peter 3:15). When we consistently live out our faith, God can use even the smallest details to reach others.

I'm reminded of this when I recall a long-ago conversation with a business associate. I casually remarked I was glad our meeting had ended earlier than planned so I could make it to Bible study that evening. Several weeks later, she asked if she could talk to me about my beliefs, having been encouraged to do so by my simple statement regarding Bible study. In time, she began attending church and made a profession of faith.

God's Fellow Workers

In his first letter to the Corinthians, the apostle Paul mentions different roles we might assume in others' spiritual journeys. God may call us to sow seeds of faith by sharing the gospel with someone who's never heard His plan of redemption. Then again, He may assign us to water those seeds already planted by coming alongside fellow believers in their walk with Him. Given Jesus' parable of the sower (Matthew 13:22), I think weeding could be added to Paul's analogy, as we help keep weeds of worry from choking fragile faith by reminding others of God's assurances and recounting His faithfulness in our lives.

Regardless of our assignment, it is a great privilege to labor in God's fields, doing our part to ensure a plentiful harvest, knowing that God is the One who brings about spiritual growth (1 Corinthians 3:5-9). Furthermore, He will see the process of sanctification through to its completion (Philippians 1:6).

I cherish the passalong plants in my garden and the friends who gave them to me. Even more, I treasure those who've planted, watered, and weeded my spiritual garden and the blessing of doing the same in the lives of my fellow sojourners.

Lord, thank You for entrusting us with the gospel message. Please help us to hold unswervingly to the hope we profess, considering how we may spur one another on toward love and good deeds as we share the hope we have in Jesus, all for Your glory.

Are You Contagious?

Set a guard, O LORD, over my mouth; keep watch over the door of my lips!
Psalm 141:3

The Blight

As part of my horticultural studies, I spent several months interning at a botanical garden near my home. Each day was different as another intern and I assisted the head gardener with whatever he needed to accomplish. Planting, pruning, weeding. We even scrubbed all the stones in the birdbath sculpture behind the house. Most of our activities were interesting, educational, and enjoyable.

However, one activity, repeated every couple of weeks throughout the summer, wasn't much fun. That task? Removing leaves affected with early blight from the tomato plants. It was a tedious process that required us to dip the blades of our pruners into alcohol after every snip of an infected leaf. Why? To decrease the possibility of spreading the disease to other areas of the plant or to other plants entirely. We also had to bag up the affected leaves and put them in the trash, not the compost bin, since blight spores can survive on plant debris, offering still other opportunities for the blight to proliferate.

Even though following the procedure took more time than clipping a succession of leaves with no dipping in between, it was worth it. It slowed the progression of the blight, enabling the tomatoes to survive and bear fruit.

Spreading Spiritual Disease

Removing diseased leaves from my own plants often reminds me of the great lengths we went to protect the tomato plants. And it leads me to contemplate the importance of removing disease-producing spores from our spiritual lives.

The habit of uttering life-taking words can be as contagious as any disease and every bit as deadly when it comes to relationships. We might like to think we're immune to such habits, but it's easy to slip into negativity and engage in gossip. We complain instead of praise. We break trust by repeating confidences shared with us. We promote ourselves. Soon diseased fruit is sprouting up around us.

Scripture vividly describes the damage inflicted by boastful, unbridled tongues that burn like unrelenting fires (James 3:5-6). Criticism, anger, lying, complaining. Left unchecked, they'll destroy the bond of unity Jesus fervently prayed for and taint our witness to a watching world (John 17:20-23).

But that's not all. By using life-taking words, we'll grieve the Holy Spirit. I find that statement to be both sobering and sad, yet the Apostle Paul says that's what we do when we engage in corrupt talk, full of wrath and malice toward others (Ephesians 4:30).

The Antidote

So how are we to keep from spreading the spores of negativity, infecting those around us? By immersing ourselves in God's Word. Just as we used alcohol to cleanse the blades of the pruners, the Spirit applies Scripture to inoculate us against unhealthy influences, to purify our thoughts and refine our intentions. For in the Bible, we see Jesus' example on glorious display. His humility (Philippians 2:3-8). His compassion (Matthew 9:36; Matthew 15:32; Luke 7:12-14). His silence before His accusers as He entrusted Himself to the One who judges justly (Isaiah 53:7; 1 Peter 2:23).

As the Spirit works to transform us more and more into the image of Christ, we're able to spread the fragrance of the knowledge of Him everywhere. And, like the tomato plants after we removed the blight, we can bear good fruit - love, joy, peace, patience, kindness, goodness, faithfulness, gentleness, self-control (Galatians 5:22-23). That sort of influence will protect the spiritual health of our fellow believers instead of infecting them with damaging discontent.

Dear Lord, please let no corrupting talk come out of our mouths, but only such as is useful for building up, that it may give grace to those who hear. May we set Your Word as a guard over our lips.

Bearing All Things

Love bears all things, believes all things, hopes all things, endures all things. Love never ends.
1 Corinthians 13:7-8

Crape Murder

One of my favorite things about living in the South is the relatively mild winters. Hints of spring appear soon after the first of the year and nudge my plant friends and me from hibernation.

Unfortunately, late winter is also when the results of crape murder confront me around every bend as I drive through my neighborhood. Oh, the carnage! I will admit to engaging in the practice, which involves severely pruning lovely crape myrtles, sometimes back to their main trunks, once after my husband Ray died.

Thankfully, I read an article by a renowned horticulturist decrying the practice before I inflicted damage a second time. Such pruning results in unsightly specimens and causes the plants to sprout weak branches at the point of the cuts.

Seeing these maimed specimens makes me cringe. However, despite being mercilessly whacked back, most crape myrtles persevere and bring forth flowers.

Persevering Through Pain

As I've observed and pondered this cycle of events year after year, it has occurred to me that some people are much like the crape myrtles. Frequently wounded and taken for granted even by those they love, they nevertheless bear the fruit of the Spirit and the sweet fragrance of life. They faithfully serve, knowing who it is they ultimately seek to please and that their labor in Him is not in vain (1 Corinthians 15:58).

Many people refer to 1 Corinthians 13 as the "Love Chapter." Verses 4 through 8 describe love as follows:

> Love is patient and kind; love does not envy or boast; it is not arrogant or rude. It does not insist on its own way; it is not irritable or resentful; it does not rejoice at wrongdoing, but rejoices with the truth. Love bears all things, believes all things, hopes all things, endures all things. Love never ends.

Many years ago, a Bible study leader suggested to our group that we try reading through these verses using our name; for example, Patsy is patient and kind, and so forth. We laughed uncomfortably, recognizing we couldn't meet those high standards, at least not consistently. Then our leader suggested we substitute "Jesus." We were quiet as we contemplated the beauty and perfection of our Savior. The passage described God's gift of love incarnate.

Our Example

Like the wounded crape myrtles, Jesus had no form or majesty that we should look at Him and no beauty that we should desire Him (Isaiah 53:2). He took on human form, not counting equality with God a thing to be grasped, but emptied Himself by taking the form of a servant, by being born in the likeness of men (Philippians 2:6-7).

Jesus bore all things, all the hardships and insults of taking on flesh. He was rejected, misunderstood, and beaten. One disciple betrayed Him with a kiss, while another denied ever being with him. Most notably, He bore our sins, enduring the cross for the joy set before Him, looking beyond the shame and pain to the glory (Hebrews 12:2). When He returns, the current world order will be turned upside down – the first shall be last, the least shall be greatest, and the meek shall inherit the earth.

As we await His promised return, we can be confident we're not alone. Even now, He is seated at the right hand of God interceding for us. Therefore, may we not grow weary in doing good, regardless of the response we receive now, knowing that in due season we will reap if we do not give up (Galatians 6:9).

O Lord, it is so hard for us to bear up under mistreatment, to love and persevere like Jesus. We want to strike back, to protect ourselves. Instead, please help us to humble ourselves under Your mighty hand as He did, knowing that you will exalt us at the proper time.

Mine!

Who has first given to me, that I should repay him? Whatever is under the whole heaven is mine.
Job 41:11

Brusque Birds

With the advent of colder weather, the activity around my birdfeeders increases, as there are fewer natural food sources available. Tufted titmice and cardinals, chickadees and nuthatches, wrens and woodpeckers are regular visitors, eagerly partaking of the sunflower seeds and suet.

Despite the increased traffic, the feeding generally proceeds harmoniously, with birds flitting from feeder to tree branch to deck railing, taking turns as it were. But occasionally, one of the diners becomes impatient. A commotion ensues as the bird abruptly flaps his way to the feeder, scattering his equally-hungry companions.

Whether patient or pushy, the birds have done nothing to earn the savory seeds. They are a gift, freely given.

Planted Together

Possessive Playmates

Each December, I witness an influx of presents at daughter Mary and son-in-law Justin's house as my three grandchildren receive gifts from their parents, grandparents, and great-grandparents. Add granddaughter Lyla's birthday presents to the mix, and there are plenty of toys to fill hours with imaginative play and help hone new skills.

It's satisfying to hear the children continue to express their gratitude for the gifts they receive, often recounting who gave them a particular item and why they like it. Yet, just like the birds' jockeying for position at the feeders, there are instances when a struggle over a particular toy disrupts playtime fun. The fought-over item usually becomes the most desirable at that moment simply because someone else was intently playing with it. One sibling will grab something from another sibling, shouting, "Mine!" Ironically, snatching the object might require them to let go of one of their sibling's new treasures.

Generous Gifter

Observing the birds' antics and the behavior of my beloved grandchildren reminds me of the sentiments expressed on Christmas cards I sent out years ago. Sigrid Undset's[1] quote on the front resonated so deeply with me I kept a card for myself:

> And when we give each other Christmas gifts in his
> name, let us remember that he has given us the sun
> and the moon and the stars, and the earth with its
> forests and mountains and oceans and all that lives

---

[1] Sigrid Undset was a Norwegian novelist. She was awarded the Nobel Prize for Literature in 1928.

and moves upon them. He has given us all green things and everything that blossoms and bears fruit and all that we quarrel about and all that we have misused. And to save us from our own foolishness, from all our sins, he came down to earth and gave us himself.

God's statement to Job in the introductory verse above affirms Sigrid's assertions, as does His proclamation recorded in Psalms:

> For every beast of the forest is mine, the cattle on a thousand hills. I know all the birds of the hills, and all that moves in the field is mine. (Psalm 50:10-11)

Lest we think His ownership extends only to things, other passages remind us we belong to Him as well:

> You shall be holy to me, for I the Lord am holy and have separated you from the peoples, that you should be mine. (Leviticus 20:26)

> Know that the LORD, he is God! It is he who made us, and we are his; we are his people, and the sheep of his pasture. (Psalm 100:3)

> But you are a chosen race, a royal priesthood, a holy nation, a people for his own possession, that you may proclaim the excellencies of him who called you out of darkness into his marvelous light. Once you were not a people, but now you are God's people; once you had not received mercy, but now you have received mercy. (1 Peter 2:9-10)

A people for His own possession purchased with the blood of His precious Son! That's who we are. Everything we have, all temporal and eternal blessings, including our salvation, are gifts graciously and freely given by our loving Father. No room for boasting or bickering or grasping. Instead, may we be ever grateful that God has called us His.

Lord, how blessed we are that You have looked at us and said, "Mine!" Please help us to remember that all we have and are is due to You and Your grace poured out upon us. May we ever sing Your praises, an overflow of thankful hearts.

The Way the World Works

For we know that the whole creation has been groaning together in the pains of childbirth until now. And not only the creation, but we ourselves, who have the firstfruits of the Spirit, groan inwardly as we wait eagerly for adoption as sons, the redemption of our bodies.
Romans 8:22-23

Predators

Gulf fritillary butterflies depend on passionflower for survival. The vigorous vine, native to the southeastern United States, is the sole food source for their caterpillars. As part of my efforts to create a pollinator oasis in my suburban neighborhood, I planted a passionflower vine by my mailbox. It took a couple of years to become established, but by the third year it was flourishing – plenty of foliage for the caterpillars to devour and lots of lovely flowers for me to enjoy.

Except I couldn't find any caterpillars.

I examined the vine every morning when I went out to collect the newspaper and every evening when I checked for mail.

No caterpillars. Then one day, I saw a tiny caterpillar in the clutches of a wasp. What did I do? I turned to Google, of course! "Do wasps eat caterpillars?" Unfortunately, they do.

I kept up my twice-daily vigil, hoping there would eventually be enough caterpillars to satisfy the wasps and still leave some to make it through their life cycle. Days passed with only an occasional sighting. Then I realized there was an army of ants busily traversing the sprawling vines. Back to Google. "Do ants eat caterpillars?" Yes, they do. By this time, my anticipation at getting to watch wave after wave of caterpillars reach maturity on my vine had given way to despair since I doubted it would be possible to get rid of the ants without negatively impacting the caterpillars.

Grandson Joshua, five years old at the time, encouraged me to find the ant mound and deal with the menacing marauders at their source. I was somewhat surprised he didn't say, "That's the way the world works, Grammie," as he often does when I mourn the fact some predator has taken down its prey. Being an avid fan of the PBS series *Wild Kratts*, Joshua is incredibly knowledgeable about a multitude of creatures. He takes the food chain in stride, knowing some animals get eaten by other animals as God provides for all of His creation.

Death Entered In

Yet the world isn't working the way God originally intended, particularly when it comes to death. Some time ago, I was reading the first chapter of Genesis, a passage I've read countless times, when I noticed something. Take a look at verses 29 and 30:

> And God said, "Behold, I have given you every plant yielding seed that is on the face of all the earth, and every tree with seed in its fruit. You shall have them for food. And to every beast of the earth and to every bird of the heavens and to everything that creeps on the earth, everything that has the breath of life, **I have given every green plant for food."** (Emphasis added.)

Do you see it too? In the beginning, when God created everything and it was all good, there was no death, not even animals eating each other. Death entered in after the fall, the penalty for disobedience (Genesis 2:16-17). I wonder what Adam and Eve thought when they saw the blood of the innocent animal God killed to supply garments of skin to cover their nakedness. What horror they must have felt when Cain killed Abel. The shedding of blood became commonplace. Sadly, that's the way the world works now.

Restoration

But the spotless Lamb of God came to save and restore by shedding His own precious blood. Without the shedding of blood, there is no forgiveness of sins (Hebrews 9:22). With it, we have the assurance that someday all things will be set right again. The world will work once more as its Creator initially intended. Speaking of Jesus' return, the prophet Isaiah wrote:

> Righteousness will be his belt and faithfulness
> the sash around his waist.
> The wolf will live with the lamb,
> the leopard will lie down with the goat,
> the calf and the lion and the yearling together;
> and a little child will lead them.

The cow will feed with the bear,
their young will lie down together,
 and the lion will eat straw like the ox.
The infant will play near the cobra's den,
and the young child will put its hand into the viper's nest.
They will neither harm nor destroy on all my holy mountain,
for the earth will be filled with the knowledge of the LORD as the waters cover the sea. (Isaiah 11:5-9) (Emphasis added.)

When I read that passage, I want to shout, "Hallelujah!" Jesus' promised return is guaranteed. We can wait confidently and expectantly for the day when death is swallowed up in victory. And while we wait, God tenderly sustains His creation.

My daily caterpillar search eventually yielded the results I'd been hoping for – a dozen or so voracious nibblers of various sizes. More followed as several generations consumed the vine. I suppose it's a small thing in the overall scheme of life. But I see it as a reminder of Christ's victory over death and the blessed restoration to come.

O Lord, how we look forward to the day of Jesus' return when the world will work again as You intended from the beginning. No more tears, no more death, no more harm on all Your holy mountain.

Letting Go

Remember not the former things, nor consider the things of old. Behold, I am doing a new thing; now it springs forth, do you not perceive it?
Isaiah 43:18-19

Coming Attractions

Over the years Ray and I were married, I saw him pull up perfectly good plants to make way for the next season's annuals. I was always appalled since I'm one of those people who doesn't like to waste anything. Yet he knew the next season's plants needed time to establish their roots and get acclimated before the upcoming season's harsher temperatures arrived, be they summer's highs or winter's lows.

As I've become more knowledgeable horticulturally, I've realized Ray was right. I try to get my cool-season annuals placed in their beds at a reasonable time, even if it means pulling up still-blooming warm-season plants and vice versa. I do, however, apologize to the plants I'm pulling up and thank them for providing so much enjoyment across their respective season.

Strength or Weakness?

A wise friend pointed out that our strengths become weaknesses when pushed to their extremes. I'm loyal and dedicated, a consummate Golden Retriever for those of you familiar with Gary Smalley and John Trent's animal-based personality profiles.[1] Furthermore, I'm not fond of change. The corporation I worked for had ten guiding principles, one of which was "embrace change." I used to joke, "Me, embrace change? No, I run the other way!" And one of my longtime friends has dubbed me the least spontaneous person she knows. You get the picture.

Just as I hesitate to remove still-flowering plants from my garden, I find it difficult to let go of people or situations, even when it would be best to do so – loyal and dedicated, to a fault.

After experiencing months of tension at work and wondering if I should resign, my 30-year career ended abruptly when my employer eliminated my job. I've said on many occasions since that I'd still be sitting in my cubicle, working away, if God hadn't made it abundantly clear that chapter of my life was over. And what an incredible adventure I would have missed had He not lovingly slammed that door and sent me on my way. I went back to school to study horticulture and became a first-time grandmother within six months of losing my job. What a joyful – and amusing – combination of events!

Pressing On

Becoming gainfully unemployed is just one of many positive, life-changing examples I can look back on. So you'd think I'd be better at letting go by now. Sadly, that's not the case.

---

[1] For more information visit smalleyinstitute.com

Probably because letting go feels too much like giving up or losing. Plus, there's the fear of the unknown. Yet I have no doubt God always knows what's next. He encourages us to forget the former things and to receive the new.

There are times when I'm so focused on the known and the present I can't perceive anything beyond an underlying sense of disquiet beckoning me to move forward. Like the changing of the seasons triggers my overhaul of the seasonal color in my flower beds, God uses those stressors to prepare me to reach for what lies ahead. Tentatively, I'll let go with one hand while keeping a tight grip with the other. But God is able to do far more than I can ask or imagine (Ephesians 3:20), so isn't it likely I'll need both hands to receive whatever it is He wants to give? Being a patient and compassionate Father, He works to loosen my grip and enable me to embrace His plan – His good and perfect plan (Jeremiah 29:11).

Letting go isn't giving up or losing. It's making way for the new.

Dear Lord, You are in the business of making all things new, including Your children. Please help us to let go of what lies behind and to press onward to You and our calling in Christ.

Cultivating Holiness

Therefore, as you received Christ Jesus the Lord, so walk in him, rooted and built up in him and established in the faith, just as you were taught, abounding in thanksgiving.
Colossians 2:6-7

Ask

If any of you lacks wisdom, let him ask God, who gives generously to all without reproach, and it will be given him. But let him ask in faith, with no doubting, for the one who doubts is like a wave of the sea that is driven and tossed by the wind.
James 1:5-6

Pesky Pillagers

Squirrels. What image comes to mind when you read that word? Cute furry critters? Persistent planters of acorns? Aerial acrobats jumping from tree to tree? I'll begrudgingly agree to those attributes, but able adversary tops my list.

It didn't take long for the squirrels residing in my woods to notice the bird feeders and suet hanging within reach from hooks attached to my deck railing. Their interest in the suet evaporated when I switched from yummy nut and berry combos to hot pepper.[1] However, the war over the seed-containing feeders rages on, as skirmishes continue between the squirrels and me.

---

[1] Birds' taste buds are different from those of mammals. They can feast on the hot pepper suet with nary a wince, unlike us – or squirrels!

Be Still

My battle strategies have evolved and include spring-loaded feeders that remain open when the light-weight birds land on them and close under the weight of the pesky pillagers. But that doesn't stop the squirrels from trying! They'll pounce from deck to feeder, attempting to break in or at least knock a few seeds out. Sometimes they'll even gnaw insistently on the cage surrounding the seed-containing cylinder.

I came downstairs one morning to find a squirrel wrapped around the feeder, head down, tail pointed skyward, trying to figure out how to get to the precious sunflower seeds within. The feeder was valiantly protecting its contents since the squirrel's bulk caused the outer sleeve to drop and close the openings, as it was designed to do.

I raised the window over the kitchen sink and shooed him away, but the sleeve didn't pop back into position. Closer inspection revealed the squirrel's determined efforts had unhooked one of the springs. I was NOT happy!

I brought the feeder inside and began to work, discouraged that my initial efforts to reattach the spring proved unsuccessful. As I tugged and fumbled with the hook, I prayed, "Please, Lord, help me fix this! It's so hard. The birds count on me to feed them."

And then I saw the obvious solution, which I'd completely overlooked in the midst of my fumbling. Within minutes, I refilled the fully-functioning feeder, returned it to its hanger on the deck, and watched the birds gather for their morning meal.

Seeking Wisdom

My relief quickly gave way to remorse as I realized how

often similar scenarios play out. Faced with a challenge or a problem to solve, I launch into self-initiated, self-sustained efforts fueled by emotion, resulting in frustration and futility. Is it just me, or do you automatically default to self-sufficiency too? I suppose it's part of our human condition, the need to feel in control, to do something.

But look again at the verses above from James. We have a Father who's told us to ask when we lack wisdom, coupled with the assurance that He'll grant our request. Yet there are times when my concerns are much more significant than a broken bird feeder, and the needed direction doesn't come as quickly. Times when I begin to behave like the wave James described, tossed about and anxious.

A friend once told me, "God doesn't play games with us. He doesn't hide His will from His children. Sometimes it just takes a while for us to see it."

I've thought of her wise words over the years when I've prayed for ongoing direction regarding difficult situations, leaning not on my own understanding but trusting God to direct my path (Proverbs 3:5-6).

After Ray died and I was raising our daughters alone, I sought the Lord's protection and provision, but above all else, I prayed for wisdom. When I didn't know which way to go or couldn't discern the best course of action and bereft of my wise, godly husband, I turned to God. He showed me time and again His promise to instruct, counsel, and watch over me is trustworthy (Psalm 32:8). It always will be, whether the trials I face are minute or mighty. He cares about them all.

Be Still

O Lord, even those of us who have walked with You for many years can sometimes slip into self-sufficiency, attempting to power through situations using our finite strength and wisdom. Please forgive us and help us to turn to You first, trusting You to provide from Your infinite well of wisdom and strength.

Superfood for the Soul

But Jesus answered, "It is written, 'Man shall not live by bread alone, but by every word that comes from the mouth of God'"
Matthew 4:4

Unequal Options

From the time he was big enough to sit in his highchair, grandson Joshua and I have enjoyed watching the birds flock to the feeder his dad had hung from their deck. Not wanting to be left out of the fun, I added "birdfeeder" to my Christmas list several years ago. My dad fulfilled my wish, launching a pastime that's given me hours of enjoyment since.

Being a novice faced with multiple options, I didn't know what kind of food to buy. I settled on a bag of Southern Regional Blend. The tagline on the bag declared, "blended to attract Southern songbirds," while another statement promised "25% sunflower plus safflower" seeds. However, a closer look at the ingredients list revealed millet to be the predominant component.

I chose a location for the feeder where I could keep an eye on it from two key vantage points: the window above the kitchen sink and my seat at the table. I filled the feeder and awaited the birds' arrival with joyful expectancy. It took a couple of days for them to notice the new food source, but one morning a red-bellied woodpecker arrived, followed by several tiny chickadees and some tufted titmice.

I mentioned my new hobby to a fellow bird-feeding friend who promptly shared some of his stash of many birds' favorite food: black oil sunflower seed. I gradually transitioned the contents of the feeder from the original blend until it contained only that delicacy. The changeover led to increased activity around the feeder and attracted a wider variety of birds.

In the years since, I've become more knowledgeable about the preferences of different birds. I've added suet, thistle seeds, and a premium blend containing peanuts and striped sunflower seeds to the bird buffet.

Soul Food

Observing my feathered visitors, I've reflected on the options available to us when it comes to nourishing our souls. We're blessed to live at a time when technology allows us to access spiritual teaching in many different ways – podcasts, blogs, and books, both printed and electronic. Yet, with such an assortment of choices available, we need to be discerning consumers.

Just like the components in the blend of seeds I originally purchased varied dramatically in nutritional value, some lessons are little more than filler. We must be careful not to feast on snack food when we require a diet of sound teaching instead. The Apostle Peter confirmed the importance of feeding our souls with the proper nourishment. He urged those who received his letter to crave pure spiritual milk, like infants hungering for their mothers' milk, that they would grow strong in their faith (1 Peter 2:2).

Praise God for providing His inerrant Word, the standard against which all other instruction is to be measured. Scripture is

- ❖ profitable for teaching, rebuking, correcting, and training in righteousness, capable of equipping us for every good work (2 Timothy 3:16-17).
- ❖ living and active, sharper than any two-edged sword, piercing to the division of soul and spirit, of joints and marrow, and discerning the thoughts and intentions of the heart (Hebrews 4:12).
- ❖ able to accomplish the purposes of God and never return to Him void (Isaiah 55:11).

Given the power of this spiritual superfood, it's no wonder Jesus deflected Satan's temptation to turn stones into bread by affirming the real source of our sustenance – every word that comes from the mouth of God.

In his second letter to Timothy, the Apostle Paul warned that a time would come when people would no longer listen to the truth but instead turn to teachers who told them what they wanted to hear (2 Timothy 4:3-4). Like my friend who enlightened me when it came to feeding the birds, may we faithfully point fellow believers to God's Word, the supreme soul food.

O Lord, how blessed we are to have Your Word to guide and sustain us! Thank You for providing many ways for us to receive spiritual nourishment. Please help us to make Your Word the benchmark against which we evaluate the nutritional value of all other sources.

Where's Your Focus?

But the Lord answered her, "Martha, Martha, you are anxious and troubled about many things, but one thing is necessary. Mary has chosen the good portion, which will not be taken away from her."
Luke 10:41-42

Focal Points

A specimen plant is used in landscaping to create a focal point. To merit such a prominent role, the plant generally has a unique or impressive attribute. I have several such plants on my property, including my beloved crape myrtle. Depending on the season, different characteristics of the stately tree command attention, including its size, exfoliating bark, and flower-laden branches. The crape myrtle is often the first thing people notice when they stop by to visit.

Just as experienced landscapers carefully select specimen plants to create garden-enhancing focal points, we need to take great care in choosing what we focus on moment by moment and day by day as we go about our lives. We're all surrounded by varying demands requiring action or decisions on our part. The weight of responsibility and pace of life can lead to a sense of disquiet and anxiety, especially if we concentrate on prevailing circumstances.

But what if we could shift our focus to something, or better yet Someone, who offers peace amidst all the hustle and bustle?

Frazzled

Jesus became friends with a fellow named Lazarus and his sisters, Martha and Mary. The Gospel of Luke recounts a visit He paid the family:

> Now as they went on their way, Jesus entered a village. And a woman named Martha welcomed him into her house. And she had a sister called Mary, who sat at the Lord's feet and listened to his teaching. But Martha was distracted with much serving. And she went up to him and said, "Lord, do you not care that my sister has left me to serve alone? Tell her then to help me." But the Lord answered her, "Martha, Martha, you are anxious and troubled about many things, but one thing is necessary. Mary has chosen the good portion, which will not be taken away from her."
> (Luke 10:38-42)

I don't know about you, but I can relate to Martha! I'm wired to work. Making to-do lists and tending to details come naturally to me. I find it challenging to sit still when there are things to be done. And it seems I can always find something that needs doing. Before I know it, I'm frazzled and grumpy, just like Martha.

An Invitation to Refocus

Can you hear the gentleness in Jesus' admonishment, though? It reminds me of His instructions to seek first His kingdom and His righteousness, and not to worry about what we'll eat or drink because He will provide these things for us as well (Matthew 6:25-33). His invitation to come to Him for rest for our souls resonates with a similar promise. His yoke is easy, and His burden is light because He bears them with us (Matthew 11:29-30).

So, does this mean we shouldn't take care of ourselves and our loved ones or tend to the details of our lives? Of course not! We'll always have responsibilities to fulfill – meals to prepare, laundry to wash and fold, bills to pay. But instead of becoming anxious and afraid, burdened and weighed down by focusing on our circumstances, we need to turn our eyes upon Jesus.

Earlier, I described a specimen plant as one that has an impressive or unique attribute. In three brief but compelling verses, the opening lines of Hebrews extol several of Jesus' matchless characteristics. He is the Son of God, heir of all things, the radiance of God's glory, an exact imprint of His nature. Not only was everything created through Him, but He also sustains all things through His powerful word. He's seated at God's right hand, having accomplished our salvation (Hebrews 1:1-3).

Jesus, our Lord and Savior, is supremely worthy to be our focal point.

Lord, we become what we behold. Please help us choose the better part as Mary did, sitting at your feet as we spend time in Your Word. For it is there we'll see You in all Your glory.

Thrashing About

And in the fourth watch of the night he came to them, walking on the sea. But when the disciples saw him walking on the sea, they were terrified, and said, "It is a ghost!" and they cried out in fear. But immediately Jesus spoke to them, saying, "Take heart; it is I. Do not be afraid." And Peter answered him, "Lord, if it is you, command me to come to you on the water." He said, "Come." So Peter got out of the boat and walked on the water and came to Jesus. But when he saw the wind, he was afraid, and beginning to sink he cried out, "Lord, save me." Jesus immediately reached out his hand and took hold of him, saying to him, "O you of little faith, why did you doubt?" And when they got into the boat, the wind ceased.
Matthew 14:25-32

I suppose I should preface this story by saying I don't consider myself to be particularly punny – that's the province of my daughter, Jessie, who inherited her dad's sense of humor – but this title, well, I couldn't resist.

Bird Behavior

Soon after I started feeding the birds, I added suet cakes to the feast I set out for them. The fat-based, high-calorie food is a favorite of woodpeckers, but it also attracts many other species.

Brown thrashers are among the larger birds that visit the suet. I find their attempts to steady themselves on the wire basket to be quite entertaining. Inevitably, when one lands on the suet, it starts to wobble. Sensing the instability of its roost, the bird flaps frantically, trying to steady itself. Its actions result in the basket spinning around, bringing about another flurry of desperate fluttering. It's a comical yet sad sight because the thrasher's behavior keeps it from the nourishment it's seeking.

Compare this to the behavior of the stately red-bellied woodpecker who frequents the suet. Every bit as big as the thrasher, he has no trouble positioning himself on the basket and consuming the nutritious treat. He doesn't anxiously beat his wings or nervously change position, even if the suet shifts slightly or he has to hang from the bottom of the basket when the suet's almost gone. The woodpecker remains calm, focused on the food before him.

Overcome By Circumstances?

The birds' behavior reminds me of Peter's attempt to walk on water, recounted in the passage above. As long as Peter kept his gaze firmly fixed on Jesus, he was able to accomplish the remarkable feat. But when he shifted his focus to the wind and waves, he was quickly overwhelmed by his situation, convinced he would drown.

I have no room to condemn Peter or the thrashers. Often, when winds of uncertainty create blustery billows, I become flustered. Like the doubting disciple and thrashing birds, I begin to flail about, thwarting any possibility of finding the stability I seek. And before I know it, I've lost sight of the One who is my sure foundation.

Preaching, Not Thrashing

Do you listen to yourself and your fears? Or, as Welsh pastor D. Martyn Lloyd-Jones admonished, do you preach to yourself, reminding yourself "who God is and what God is and what God has done and what God has pledged Himself to do?"[1]

When I feel myself beginning to go under, I use a simple phrase, inspired by watching the birds: "No thrashing!" It helps me look beyond my circumstances to see my Savior, His hand extended, ready to steady me in the storm.

As I've continued to observe them, I've noticed the thrashers have become more adept at landing on the suet. They occasionally extend a wing to balance themselves, but panicked flapping is rare. They've learned to keep their eyes on the target before them.

Lord, please help us keep our eyes fixed on You, remembering You are our Rock and Refuge, a calm sanctuary in turbulent times.

---

[1] D. Martyn Lloyd-Jones, *Spiritual Depression: Its Causes and Cures*, Eerdmans Publishing Company, 1965.

The Imposter

[Satan] was a murderer from the beginning, and does not stand in the truth, because there is no truth in him. When he lies, he speaks out of his own character, for he is a liar and the father of lies.
John 8:44

What's That?!

My garden is home to a stand of native columbines, offspring of plants my late husband started over 20 years ago. Like many other gardening tasks, ensuring the columbines' survival was something I had to learn by doing after Ray passed away suddenly one warm April evening. As I cut back the spent flowers later that spring, I realized they were laden with seeds. Many spurted out when I cut the dried stems, dotting the ground and decorating my shirt. I decided to sprinkle more around for good measure. And sprinkle I did, shaking pod after pod of dried columbines!

Months passed. Raising two young daughters alone and trying to find my footing in a world turned upside down consumed much of my time and energy. But winter waned, warmer days returned, and the garden beckoned me. A reconnaissance stroll yielded several encouraging finds – tiny plants emerging from their winter slumber. "Hmm," I wondered. "What could all those leaves springing up in the front bed be?"

Then I remembered scattering columbine seeds everywhere. It worked! I've continued the sprinkling tradition ever since, and each year I've been blessed with a bumper crop.

When I was first taking stock of the returning plants, I noticed some leaves that looked almost like columbine foliage with a similar growth habit. Not wanting to pull up desirable plants, I decided to let them develop until I was sure. Big mistake! By the time I discerned they were weeds, they'd put down roots, matured, and reproduced. The imposters return each spring alongside the columbines, hiding out, hoping I won't spot them. But after two decades of careful observation and informed scrutiny, I'm able to readily detect the difference, even when the plants are still tiny. I pluck the weeds before they have a chance to get established and take over valuable garden real estate.

Fake Friend

Like my early dealings with the weeds, it's easy to let questionable behavior or ungodly thoughts gain a foothold. We rationalize, "Looks like a good thing. I'm not sure, but it won't hurt to try it out, at least until I know. I can redirect later if need be."

By the time we recognize the situation for what it is, it's much more challenging to handle than if we'd been more spiritually vigilant from the start. Unlike the weeds which aren't, in reality, out to get me, we have an adversary bent on our destruction. Though he knows his ultimate defeat is certain, he prowls about like a roaring lion seeking whom he may destroy (1 Peter 5:8). He masquerades as an angel of light (2 Corinthians 11:14), tempting with promises that seem oh-so-reasonable, all while discounting potentially deadly consequences. He's used the same tactics since he first appeared on the scene (Genesis 3:1-5).

Practicing Discernment

Fortunately, there is a way to resist him. We must draw near to God, making use of the mighty armor He provides for us. Ephesians 6 describes the Word of God as the sword of the Spirit. We are to use it to protect our thoughts and to fend off lies. When we think on God's powerful Word, we are enabled more and more to test and approve what His will is – His good, pleasing, and perfect will (Romans 12:2).

As the colony of columbines has become increasingly dominant over the years, there's less room for the annoying intruders. Those that do appear don't get to stay around long since I can now readily identify them. Just as I've consistently sprinkled columbine seeds and studied the resulting plants' appearance, let us liberally sow God's truth in our lives and meditate on its teachings. In so doing, may we more easily recognize the Father of Lies and weed out his wily temptations before they have a chance to entice and entangle us.

Thank You, Lord, for Your Word. Please help us to look into it deeply and frequently so that we're able to discern the difference between truth and deception.

Don't Tempt Me

Therefore let anyone who thinks that he stands take heed lest he fall.
1 Corinthians 10:12

No Arm-Twisting Needed

I'm a list maker. I like to write out my chores, then cross them off one by one as I finish them. Several years ago, I woke up determined to tackle a list of indoor tasks, but radiant sunshine greeted me. I checked the forecast. Yes! Afternoon temps in the 60s; one of those warm mid-winter days we can look forward to in the South. My trusty to-do list, once a facilitator to accomplishing my goals for the day, became an obstacle to fulfilling my budding desire to spend time outside.

I had an internal debate with myself as I prepared breakfast. Should I stick with my original plan and get my work done or permit myself to go outside and indulge in one of my favorite activities? Decisions, decisions. Knowing how much I enjoy working in my yard, a friend suggested I postpone my chores and spend at least a few moments outside. Furthermore, he pointed out the extended forecast was calling for clouds the next day, followed by rain the next. Perfect! Just what I needed – someone to support me in going with Plan B.

When I got dressed for the day, I put on a pair of old jeans I reserve for working outside in case I decided to enjoy those few moments. Shortly after noon, I went to get the mail. That did it. The warmth of the sun melted any sliver of resolve I might have been holding onto regarding sticking to my original plan.

I ate lunch, happily anticipating the outdoor moments I was going to allow myself. Those moments turned into over 2 ½ hours. I could make a persuasive argument that my garden and I both benefitted from the time I spent outside. After all, I consider gardening to be one of the best forms of therapy, and weeds had almost taken over the front bed, encouraged into proliferation by our abnormally warm weather.

Slippery Slope

As I knelt pulling up handfuls of chickweed, I couldn't help but think how easy it is to rationalize giving in to our desires. Even when we know what God requires of us and the stakes are much higher than not getting our chores done. Even when we believe He established boundaries because He loves us and knows what's best for us.

God's children rarely leap from obedience to egregious sin in one step. As James described, it's a process:

> But each person is tempted when he is lured and enticed by his own desire. Then desire when it has conceived gives birth to sin, and sin when it is fully grown brings forth death. (James 1:14-15)

Cultivating Holiness

It's a progression that's been repeated countless times since Satan deceived Eve. We see, we ponder, we act. And sometimes we act repeatedly, moving further and further down a path we never intended to take.

Such was the case with King David. 2 Samuel 11 recounts the sordid affair, which began when David didn't accompany his troops into battle. Back at home, while strolling on his rooftop, he spied beautiful Bathsheba taking a bath. Did he respectfully avert his eyes? Nope. He allowed his gaze to linger. Thus ignited, his passion eventually led him to commit adultery and murder. He was the King, a man after God's own heart, but his desire got the best of him.

The Way Back

Confronted by the prophet Nathan, David repented, overcome by his sin (Psalm 51). God forgave and cleansed him, as He's promised to do whenever we seek His forgiveness. Even so, David's blatant disregard of God's commands resulted in severe consequences (2 Samuel 12:10-14).

And so it is with our sin. We can count on God to call us back from our wanderings and to forgive us, yet there are consequences, part of our Father's loving discipline. How much better to remember we are susceptible to temptation and to look to God for strength to resist before we take even the first step down the wayward path (1 Corinthians 10:13).

Lord, please help us not to get carried away by our desires, but to avail ourselves of the means of escape You provide. May we draw near to You, knowing You will draw near to us.

Weeds

A sower went out to sow. And as he sowed, some seeds fell along the path, . . . Other seeds fell among thorns, and the thorns grew up and choked them.
Matthew 13:3-4, 7

Weeding – the mere thought of spending time plucking unwanted plant intruders from your garden may make some of you shudder. But I usually don't mind the chore, especially when the soil is moist and the weather is pleasant. My mind can wander while my hands are busy, and I take satisfaction in seeing the results of my efforts. Desirable plants, previously hidden beneath the unwelcome ones, become visible once freed from the encroachers' stranglehold.

In Matthew 13, Jesus compares the different outcomes of seeds sown in varying soil conditions to the relative success of the Word of God taking root in someone's life. Likewise, I've come to regard sin as the spiritual equivalent of weeds as they impede the growth of our relationship with God and others.

Maybe you'll think of sin that way, too, after you read through the following comparisons!

Stubborn Roots

Perseverance, one of the qualities I most admire about plants, isn't quite as endearing when exhibited by the ones I don't want in my garden. Some weeds have a long taproot that makes them incredibly difficult to eradicate. They may disappear for a season or two, but if you leave part of the root, the weed will eventually return – often more robust than before.

Dealing with sin often requires addressing not only the presenting behavior but also the thoughts and attitudes which led to it in the first place. Like ridding our gardens of weeds that grow from taproots, we can't eradicate deep-seated sins until we do the hard work of digging the tough roots out of our hearts, roots like anger, bitterness, and unforgiveness (Ephesians 4:30-32).

Dormant Seeds

Other weeds have shallow roots, but if you don't remove the plants before they mature and set seed, you might find yourself dealing with their progeny for years to come. Some weed seeds can lie dormant for as long as 50 years, and then, when exposed to just the right conditions, they germinate, leaving an unsuspecting gardener to wonder what happened.

Most of us have at least one area where we're particularly vulnerable to temptation, an area where we need to remain extra-vigilant. Like the seeds that lie dormant waiting for the right conditions, old habits may return if we become complacent. Even worse, after a period of success in dealing with a particular sin, we may think we've become immune to the temptation and naively place ourselves in situations where we're sure to fail (1 Corinthians 10:12).

Painful Thorns

And then there are briars and thistles, so prickly they can cause physical harm to those not adequately equipped to confront them. Anyone who's unknowingly grabbed Smilax with an ungloved hand can attest to the fact it deserves its common name, cat briar. The scratches it leaves on unprotected flesh are similar to those you would expect from an encounter with an angry feline.

The appealing qualities of sin can hide the dangerous thorns, at least until we clutch the forbidden fruit. Whether the pain is immediate or develops over time as the barbs cut into our souls, it is inevitable for God's children. Our loving Father disciplines us, for we are to be holy as He is holy (Hebrews 12:11).

Overwhelming Overgrowth

Weeds compete with desirable plants for water and nutrients. They can even prevent light from reaching them if left long enough to form a dense, matted tangle. I've learned it's more effective to do battle early and often than trying to remove weeds several weeks after their appearance. When weather conditions or busyness keeps me from doing so, I often lament, "There are so many weeds, it looks like I planted them on purpose!" More than once, I've had to enlist help to restore order to the overgrown mess.

Sin can choke out joy and spiritual growth as it entangles us and blocks the Light we need to flourish. Sometimes we can get so far off track spiritually we need help and support to stay the course until we've returned to the narrow way. At such times, prayer warriors and accountability partners are invaluable as they help us carry our burden (Galatians 6:1-2).

Dear Lord, just as we have an ongoing battle with the weeds in our gardens, we must remain vigilant to weed out sin in our lives. Thank You that we don't battle alone but have the power of the Spirit at work within us, helping us want to obey You and helping us to do your will.

Transformation

And we know that for those who love God all things work together for good, for those who are called according to his purpose. For those whom he foreknew he also predestined to be conformed to the image of his Son, in order that he might be the firstborn among many brothers. And those whom he predestined he also called, and those whom he called he also justified, and those whom he justified he also glorified.
Romans 8:28-30

Soul Amendments

And I will give you a new heart, and a new spirit I will put within you. And I will remove the heart of stone from your flesh and give you a heart of flesh. And I will put my Spirit within you, and cause you to walk in my statutes and be careful to obey my rules.
Ezekiel 36:26-27

Unfriendly Ground

When we moved from Delaware to Georgia, we had the opportunity to start from the ground up. We chose our lot, chose a house plan, chose a builder. After years of working as a color developer and carpet stylist for a large corporation, I enthusiastically put my job experience into practice. I selected all the finishes for the house – from bricks to shingles, wall colors to carpet – and amassed a burgeoning file of paint chips and swatches. My late husband, Ray, was equally excited about using his horticulture training in designing our landscape. His task proved to be much more challenging than mine.

For starters, most of the topsoil had been scraped away by bulldozers cruising back and forth, grading the site. Compacted

Georgia clay – think terra cotta pottery – remained in its place. I watched as Ray struggled to dig holes in the hardened ground, thinking he might as well have been chipping away at the concrete driveway.

Next, there was the appalling but legal practice of burying construction debris on the property. Among our stranger discoveries – the lid to a 5-gallon paint bucket and a caulking gun containing a half-empty caulk canister.

And then there were rocks to deal with, some too big to dig up, others temporary yet annoying obstacles. The distinct clang of the shovel hitting their unyielding surfaces accompanied Ray's efforts to install the carefully-chosen plants.

Amended Soil

Born and raised in South Dakota farm country, Ray was accustomed to soil so rich it's nearly black. When we lived in Delaware, we would occasionally get a load of mushroom compost to top-dress the yard – smelly but effective when it came to adding nutrients to the soil. These experiences, plus his horticulture degree, informed Ray there would be no shortcut when it came to improving the hardpan he'd inherited. Thus he began the tedious process of amending the clay by tilling in topsoil and compost.

But was it ever worth it!

Now, almost 30 years later, the soil is dark, easy to dig, and full of busy earthworms, a sure sign of health. When I cultivate those beds, my thoughts often drift to the early days when the daunting conditions hindered Ray's landscaping efforts. Nonetheless, he persevered, patiently applying the principles he knew would yield the longed-for results.

Receptive Hearts

In the Parable of the Sower,[1] Jesus described different classes of soils and compared them to one's ability to accept and nurture the seed of gospel truth. Just like Ray worked to remove the unyielding rocks and clay from our flower beds to create welcoming plots for our plants, God replaces our stony hearts with hearts of flesh to enable us to welcome the gospel. Thus prepared, our hearts can yield a bountiful harvest of righteousness like the good soil in Jesus' parable, as the Spirit oversees and empowers our growth.

When I went back to school to study horticulture, I gained a whole new appreciation for soil. Structure, drainage, nutrient-holding capacity – all are important in determining what kind of life it can support. Though the heart exchange is a once-and-done event, the tending will continue until we're called Home. With the Spirit's help, we're to amend our softened hearts with the Word, working it into our lives. Then our roots will have room to grow, penetrating deeply into nourishing truth. We'll be like the trees planted by streams of water described in Jeremiah 17:8 – unafraid of drought and consistently bearing fruit.

There will undoubtedly be rocks and debris for us to remove as we dig deeper into our souls, stumbling blocks to our spiritual growth. Here too, we can depend on the Spirit to aid our efforts as He conforms us to the likeness of Christ (Romans 8:29).

How about you? Are you amending the soil of your soul with the life-giving, life-sustaining Word of God?

---

[1] Matthew 13:1-8, 18-23; Mark 4:3-8, 14-20; Luke 8:5-8, 11-15.

Be Still

Lord, thank You for removing our hearts of stone and replacing them with hearts of flesh, receptive ground for the seeds of life and hope that You plant within us.

Prudent Pruning

I am the true vine, and my Father is the vinedresser. Every branch in me that does not bear fruit he takes away, and every branch that does bear fruit he prunes, that it may bear more fruit.
John 15:1-2

Beneficial Pruning

Pruning requires skill and an understanding of the plant being pruned. Some plants bloom on old wood, others on new. Some require severe pruning to increase fruitfulness, while such treatment will stunt, disfigure, or kill others.

As much as I decry the practice of crape murder, I recognize the need for proper pruning. Done correctly, it is an essential part of maintaining a specimen's health and enhancing its aesthetic value.

After some years of practice, I feel more confident when it comes time to trim my trees and shrubs, yet I still approach the task with a measure of trepidation. What if the results of my efforts look more like a bad haircut? Or I snip off next year's buds? Or I accidentally remove the flowering branch instead of the dead one next to it because the shrub was so thick I didn't have a clear view? Yep, I've found myself in those situations – more than once. And I've learned to call for professional help when the job is too big or too complicated for me to handle.

Spiritual Pruning

The introductory verses above from the Gospel of John are familiar. Removing dead branches and those that aren't bearing fruit seems reasonable—but pruning the fruitful ones to make them more fruitful? Increasing by taking away sounds counterintuitive until you understand the science behind the analogy. Without delving too deeply into the details, pruning stimulates plant growth at the point of the cut by removing growth-inhibiting hormones present in the tips of branches and stems.

So what might pruning look like in the spiritual realm given we're to produce fruit in keeping with repentance, fruit that provides evidence of our faith?

- ❖ Loss leads to empathy for others experiencing similar losses. I've often said that before Ray died, I was genuinely sorry for those who lost a beloved spouse, but after losing him, I became intimately acquainted with the sorrow associated with such a blow. My sympathy became empathy, which in turn has allowed me to comfort others with the comfort I've received from the Lord (2 Corinthians 1:3-4).
- ❖ Trials produce patience and strengthen our faith as we wait on the Lord. As the Apostle Paul wrote in his letter to the Romans, "[W]e rejoice in our sufferings, knowing that suffering produces endurance, and endurance produces

Transformation

character, and character produces hope, and hope does not put us to shame" (Romans 5:3-5). That's a bountiful harvest of desirable traits! Furthermore, we can encourage others by stewarding our stories well, sharing examples of God's love and faithfulness.

- ❖ Discipline engenders repentance, which yields the fruit of righteousness and, later, humility. We recognize no one is righteous apart from Christ (Romans 3:10). We're to take the log out of our own eye before dealing with the speck in others', and to forgive as God has forgiven us (Matthew 7:3-5; Colossians 3:13).

Think back over your life. Were there times when God removed something or someone, resulting in an abundance of spiritual fruit?

Proper pruning, even the most severe that leaves the plant looking like a shadow of its former self, doesn't hurt the plant. Fortunately, we belong to the Master Vinedresser, not a weekend warrior wielding a chainsaw. He determines exactly where and how to make the required cuts to enable us to bear more fruit for Him. Sometimes the pruning is relentless, and the process is painful, but we can always trust Him. He knows us by name and loves us far more than we can imagine. He's tenderly transforming us into who He created us to be.

O Lord, trials, loss, discipline – the very thought makes us tremble. But we know we can trust You to bring joy from suffering, beauty from ashes, and life from death.

Bearing Fruit

For no good tree bears bad fruit, nor again does a bad tree bear good fruit, for each tree is known by its own fruit. For figs are not gathered from thornbushes, nor are grapes picked from a bramble bush. The good person out of the good treasure of his heart produces good, and the evil person out of his evil treasure produces evil, for out of the abundance of the heart his mouth speaks.
Luke 6:43-45

Identifying Features

Before I studied horticulture, I tried to identify trees by their leaves. Don't get me wrong; leaves are indispensable identifiers for many species. But they can be misleading in others. When botanists classify plants, they look instead at their reproductive structures – flowers, fruit, and seeds.

Although oak leaves come in different shapes, all oaks sprout from acorns. Likewise, there are numerous forms of maple leaves, not just the classic silhouette that appears on the Canadian flag. But all maple seeds are borne in samaras, those little winged carriers that float to the ground like tiny helicopters.

Transformation

Once I learned this, it became a fun game to see if I could spot similarities between plants at the botanical garden where I volunteer. I first noted the flowers on Abutilon with their crepe paper-like petals resemble dwarf hibiscus blossoms. Despite the shape of its leaves, which leads to one of its common names, flowering maple, Abutilon is part of the Malvaceae family, as are hibiscus and okra. (Check out the gorgeous flowers on the latter sometime.)

Next, I noticed the tiny white bell-shaped flowers on *Pieris japonica* look like those on a small tree known as farkleberry, and both resemble those on blueberry bushes. Those three belong to the Ericaceae family.

The more I studied, the easier it became to see the distinguishing characteristics and successfully match plants with their relatives. I wondered why I found it to be so gratifying, musing that it must be because family, both biological and spiritual, is so important to me.

Family Resemblance

Just like we can recognize plants by their fruit, Jesus taught that members of His family would bear distinguishing fruit as well, and He made it clear the only way to bear abundant spiritual fruit was to abide in Him:

> Abide in me, and I in you. As the branch cannot bear fruit by itself, unless it abides in the vine, neither can you, unless you abide in me. I am the vine; you are the branches. Whoever abides in me and I in him, he it is that bears much fruit, for apart from me you can do nothing. John 15:4-5

I'm frequently reminded of His statement when I'm pruning. I sometimes leave piles of discarded branches on the ground and then go back to collect them after I finish cutting. Inevitably, the leaves on the severed limbs are already beginning to wilt. The longer the time apart from their source of nourishment and the hotter the day, the quicker their demise. They can no longer live, much less produce fruit.

When I think of abiding, I think of peace – no striving or struggling. The word appears ten times in verses 4 to 10 of John 15, emphasizing the permanence of our relationship with Christ as well as the eternal significance of the fruit we bear. Securely connected to the Giver of Life, His life flows through us to bless and benefit others, all to the praise of His glory.

Distinctive Fruit

And what kind of distinct fruit do we produce when we abide in Him? Love, joy, peace, patience, goodness, kindness, gentleness, faithfulness, self-control (Galatians 5:22-23). All are marks of God's children, but one outshines them all – love. Jesus prayed that the love He and the Father shared would dwell richly in His followers (John 17:26). That singular mark of distinction would allow all people to identify them as members of God's family (John 13:35).

He also warned against false prophets, those seeking to deceive. Like leaves that mimic those of other plants, their outward appearance may initially camouflage their deceit. But closer inspection of the fruit borne of the evil intent in their hearts will give them away, ultimately leading to their destruction (Matthew 7:15-20).

Transformation

Not so the children of God who bear fruit in keeping with repentance and shine as lights in this dark world.

O Lord, what a privilege it is to be a branch on Your family tree. We bear the imprint of the true Vine, whose life in us allows us to bear abundant fruit of eternal value.

Exfoliation

[You] were taught in him, as the truth is in Jesus, to put off your old self, which belongs to your former manner of life and is corrupt through deceitful desires, and to be renewed in the spirit of your minds, and to put on the new self, created after the likeness of God in true righteousness and holiness.
Ephesians 4:21-24

Informed Choices

Throughout most of the years I worked for a large corporation, I held the role of colorist. As such, I developed, named, and presented new carpet color options to our customers. After all the time spent honing my abilities at work, I eagerly embraced the opportunity to select the interior and exterior colors when we built our home in Georgia.

My husband Ray's specialty, horticulture, was an equally creative endeavor. I didn't realize how I'd narrowed his flowering plant possibilities when I picked a terra cotta color scheme for the bricks and shutters, especially when it came to choosing the requisite southern plant on our list – a crape myrtle.

Transformation

Being a skilled horticulturist, Ray made an excellent choice. Unlike other crape myrtle cultivars whose pink or purple flowers would have offended my color sensibilities as they clashed with our cinnamon-colored exterior, the stately 'Natchez'[1] bears creamy-white blossoms. They create a floriferous and harmonious cascade each summer. But the brilliance of Ray's choice is most apparent in the fall when the tree's annual process of exfoliation occurs.

As summer wanes, cracks begin to appear in the bark along the mighty trunk, signaling the coming changes. Soon the cracks turn into fissures, and the old skin lifts away from the tree before finally letting go completely, falling to the ground in long jagged shards. To the uninitiated observer, this series of events may be unsettling. How could such a progression possibly be beneficial for the plant? Yet that very act allows the trunk to increase its girth and grow stronger. Best of all, it reveals the most magnificent cinnamon-colored covering. Ray saw the potential in the sapling he planted so long ago. He knew what it could become.

Put Off/Put On

There are several concepts that I consider to be spiritual touchstones. One such idea is that of putting off and putting on. Jesus made it clear in His pronouncement of woes on the Pharisees that it's not enough to make a show of getting rid of sinful thoughts and behavior (Matthew 23:25-28). Instead, our repentance must be true, the kind that produces fruit in keeping with our profession of faith, as we put on right-thinking and conduct pleasing to God.

---

[1] Lagerstroemia indica x fauriei 'Natchez'

The Apostle Paul affirms this teaching in his letter to the Romans. He encourages his readers not to conform to the world but to be transformed by the renewing of their minds (Romans 12:2). And in his letter to the Ephesians, he goes even further. After urging them to put off the old self and to put on the new in the introductory passage above, Paul goes on to provide specific examples of behavior to put off as well as corresponding replacements:

- ❖ Put away falsehood and speak the truth (v. 25).
- ❖ Let the thief no longer steal but perform honest labor (v. 28).
- ❖ Do not use unwholesome language, but that which benefits and builds up those who listen (v. 29).
- ❖ Put away all bitterness, wrath, anger, and every form of malice. Be kind to one another, forgiving one another as God in Christ forgave you (vv. 31-32).

Because of Jesus' sacrifice on our behalf, God already sees His righteousness when He looks at us (2 Corinthians 5:21), but there is much refining left to be done. We are not yet holy as He is Holy, nor will our makeover be complete until He returns. The Spirit is at work in us, sanctifying us with the same mighty power that raised Jesus from the dead (Ephesians 1:19-20).

There are times when our refinement is painful as the Helper strips away bits of our old nature. The process may cause outside observers or even believers themselves to question God's methods, especially when they involve loss and suffering. But we can trust Him to have a good and perfect plan to transform us, thereby revealing more and more of who we are in Christ.

Transformation

Just as Ray knew what the crape myrtle could become, given sufficient time and proper care, God knows who He created us to be and has promised to complete the work He's begun in us.

O Lord, how I look forward to Your return! On that glorious day, our transformation will be complete, and all vestiges of our former selves will be gone. We will gather around Your throne, our new selves robed in white, to forever praise You, our Redeemer King.

Seasons

For everything there is a season, and a time for every matter under heaven: a time to be born, and a time to die; a time to plant, and a time to pluck up what is planted; a time to kill, and a time to heal; a time to break down, and a time to build up; a time to weep, and a time to laugh; a time to mourn, and a time to dance; a time to cast away stones, and a time to gather stones together; a time to embrace, and a time to refrain from embracing; a time to seek, and a time to lose; a time to keep, and a time to cast away; a time to tear, and a time to sew; a time to keep silence, and a time to speak; a time to love, and a time to hate; a time for war, and a time for peace.
Ecclesiastes 3:1-8

Nature's Seasons

I once attended a presentation where the speaker began with, "Summer, fall, and winter are seasons – spring is a miracle." I've thought about her comment every spring since. Early warm spells begin to nudge plants from their winter sleep in January here in the South. Witchhazel, Lenten roses, and paperbush start

Transformation

the floral parade that continues for multiple weeks as plants take turns in the spotlight. Trees, flowers, baby birds – all embody the joyful message of rebirth, which in turn stimulates hope and rejuvenation in us.

But spring gives way to summer, and tender ephemerals disappear for another year as heat-loving specimens flourish. Summer annuals and perennials bloom, then set and disperse their seeds before beginning their decline. Fall arrives. Crops are ripe for harvest, the fruit of spring planting and summer tending. Soon daylight hours decrease, as does the temperature, and autumnal leaves create a riotous display of color – one last hurrah before they let go and blanket the ground for the winter.

Ah, winter. Based on my observations, I've concluded it is the most misunderstood, under-appreciated season, at least from a gardening standpoint. Those unfamiliar with the ways of plants scan the leafless, apparently lifeless landscape and pronounce, "everything's dead." I used to think that too, but my horticulture studies dissuaded me from that notion. For instance, some seeds won't germinate without scarification,[1] some bulbs won't bloom without adequate chill time, and many plants depend on the decreased daylight and increased darkness that accompany winter to flower at the appropriate time.

That knowledge has given me a different perspective. Now when I survey winter vistas, I imagine the plants are enjoying their winter slumber, building reserves for the next season of fruitfulness. Branches bearing dormant buds carry the promise of new life when spring returns.

---

[1] Scarification involves weakening, opening, or otherwise altering the coat of a seed to encourage germination.

Seasons of the Soul

Contemplating the bedraggled state of my summer annuals one early-September day reminded me of a book I'd been reading. Instead of equating the aging process with seasons as is often done, author Mark Buchanan explores what he's deemed "cycles in our hearts." In *Spiritual Rhythm, Being with Jesus Every Season of Your Soul,* he describes different periods in our lives in terms of the four seasons, each with its own set of challenges and blessings, each necessary if we're to bear fruit.

The friends who gave me the book thought the analogy would resonate with me because of my love of gardening. And so it does. Year after year, I've observed and anticipated the changes, as one season follows another, each dependent on the ones that precede.

Sometimes I think it would be nice to live in a constant state of springtime, emotionally and spiritually speaking – productive, energetic, surrounded by resurgent, hope-producing, joy-filled circumstances. But like the plants, God knows we need all the seasons to produce abundant fruit and to become more like Jesus.

We need to slow down and be still, to rest and draw near to God in all seasons, but we're most likely to do so during the winters of our souls – times of loss and suffering. For it's then we realize our utter reliance upon God, a dependence present every moment, but most evident when we come to the end of our supposed self-sufficiency.

My own winters have convinced me of the veracity of Elisabeth Elliot's declaration, "The deepest things that I have

Transformation

learned in my own life have come from the deepest suffering. And out of the deepest waters and the hottest fires have come the deepest things that I know about God."[1]

Yet, like the trees and flowers, I've emerged able to bear more fruit because I know my Father and His ways more intimately. Signs of life return as our winter gives way to another cycle of spring planting, summer tending, fall harvesting, a cycle that will continue in us and the natural world until our final winter. Our bodies will rest in the ground, waiting for reunion with our souls when we're called Home, glorified, and welcomed into the joy of eternal spring (1 Thessalonians 4:13-16).

Dear Lord, just as we savor the changing of the seasons in the natural world, please help us to embrace the seasons of our souls, knowing that You have a purpose and plan for each as the cycles of our lives continue until Jesus' return.

---

[1] Elisabeth Elliot, "Suffering is Never for Nothing," lecture series, 1989.

A Tale of Three Trees

The Lord has anointed me to bring good news to the poor; he has sent me to bind up the brokenhearted, . . . to grant to those who mourn in Zion—to give them a beautiful headdress instead of ashes, the oil of gladness instead of mourning, the garment of praise instead of a faint spirit.
Isaiah 61:1, 3

Walking the Property

A year or so after we moved to Georgia, my husband Ray and I began a tradition we called "walking the property." Let me dispel any notion you may have about us owning a vast estate. No, our property situated in a typical suburban housing development outside Atlanta, measures approximately 1/3 of an acre.

Ray had a horticulture degree with an emphasis on woody ornamentals, so he asked the builder to leave as many trees as possible when he cleared the property to make room for our home. In the five years we lived there together, Ray installed numerous unique plants whose names he patiently taught me. Although I received a degree in fashion merchandising, I loved

Transformation

plants and being outside and spending time with Ray; thus, I looked forward to our rambles and Ray's lessons.

Warmth and copious signs of spring accompanied the evening of April 16, 1997. Ray dropped Jessie and Mary, our then seven- and ten-year-old daughters, off at church for their mid-week children's activities. When he returned, we started our evening stroll at the left front corner of our house, ambled through the woods, up the other side, and back to the driveway.

Ray stopped repeatedly along our route. He pointed out plants of interest, mentioned specific landscaping plans, and commented on the health of things he'd planted in the much-amended Georgia clay. We paused by a grove of three bald cypress trees. All these years later, I don't remember how tall the juvenile trees were, probably not much taller than Ray, but I distinctly remember his comments:

"These are some of my favorite trees. They're interesting because they lose their needles."

I didn't know it would be the last time we'd walk the property. But God did.

Three nights later, my young daughters and I received life-shattering news: Ray, a mere 39 years old, had a fatal heart attack at work. He wouldn't be coming home. Ever.

Baby Trees

Over two decades have passed since that last stroll and the unthinkable loss. I focused on raising my daughters, finished a 30-year career at a large corporation, welcomed three grandchildren. Along the way, gardening became my therapy, a connection to

Be Still

Ray and to my loving heavenly Father.

And, amazingly, I got to go back to school to study horticulture! In my woody identification class, I learned there are hardly any conifers[1] that lose their needles: dawn redwood, a few larch species, and bald cypress – confirmation of Ray's long-ago statement.

The small specimens he planted now tower high above the back corner of my house. Each fall, their needles create a brilliant color display – a blaze of copper, bronze, and burnished gold – before they let go, drift to the ground, and blanket the bed beneath their intertwined branches. I've thought so often about Ray's comments and how unusual the trees are.

Five years ago, I noticed multiple seedlings peeking through the mantle of fallen needles. Upon closer inspection, I deduced they were baby bald cypresses! I contacted a friend well-versed in all things coniferous. His comment upon hearing the news: "Bald cypresses don't usually reproduce like that. They must be happy trees."

I beamed at hearing this, adding to myself, "Well-loved, too."

I dug up several of the seedlings and potted them in individual containers. In the subsequent seasons, I watered, watched, and worried them along, hoping at least three of them – one for each grandchild – would make it. And make it they did. In Fall 2019, we moved them to Mary and Justin's house. With the help of a friend, the children planted the offspring of their grandfather's favorite conifers.

---

[1] In basic terms, conifers are plants that bear their seeds in cones.

Transformation

Beauty for Ashes

The mind's eye images of that gorgeous afternoon – cloudless azure sky, warm-for-November breeze, dirty hands, and delighted laughter – are underscored by a snippet of lyrics from the hymn "Day by Day," whose first stanza reads as follows:

> Day by day and with each passing moment,
> Strength I find to meet my trials here;
> Trusting in my Father's wise bestowment,
> I've no cause for worry or for fear.
> He whose heart is kind beyond all measure
> Gives unto each day what He deems best –
> Lovingly, its part of pain and pleasure,
> Mingling toil with peace and rest. [1]

Oh, how I wish Ray were here to be Grandpa Kuipers to our grandchildren. I mourn the fact he isn't. But even at their tender ages, Joshua, Lyla, and Emma are old enough to understand the concept of having a grandfather in heaven. I speak about him often, recounting his strong faith and his love of people and plants.

When I took my last stroll with Ray, I didn't know the day would come when I'd be blessed to have three grandchildren, much less that we'd get to plant progeny of the very trees Ray had singled out that night. But God did.

O Father, thank You for sprinkling good gifts along our way to soften the blows and smooth the sharp edges of life in this world. You are faithful to redeem our losses and bring beauty from ashes.

---

[1] "Day by Day," lyrics by Carolina Sandell Berg; translated by Andrew L. Skoog.

When We Least Expect It

The Lord is not slow to fulfill his promise as some count slowness, but is patient toward you, not wishing that any should perish, but that all should reach repentance. But the day of the Lord will come like a thief, and then the heavens will pass away with a roar, and the heavenly bodies will be burned up and dissolved, and the earth and the works that are done on it will be exposed. . . . according to his promise we are waiting for new heavens and a new earth in which righteousness dwells.
2 Peter 3:9-10, 13

Surprise!

It caught my eye as soon as I pulled into the driveway, weary from a long drive home after a week at the beach. So much time had passed since the cream-colored Lycoris[1] bloomed, I didn't even remember it was there. Yet despite its long absence, in a perfectly-timed reappearance, it provided a cheerful, "Welcome home!" The fact it sprouted from a bulb planted by my late husband, Ray, over two decades prior, made its return even

---

[1] *Lycoris albiflora.*

sweeter.

The intriguing inflorescence showed up again the next year, accompanied a week or so later by another long-forgotten specimen in an adjacent flower bed. The red-flowered ones[1] took their time, showing up several weeks later. No wonder "surprise lily" is one of Lycoris' common names![2]

Be Prepared!

In the verses above, the Apostle Peter references Jesus' statement that His promised return will be a surprise. In fact, Jesus said no one knows the day or hour except the Father (Matthew 24:36). After making this statement, He went on to tell several parables, emphasizing the importance of being watchful and ready:

- ❖ First, there's the tale of the master of the house who would have stayed awake to protect his dwelling from a break-in had he known when the thief would arrive (Matthew 24:43-44).
- ❖ Then there's the story contrasting the behavior of faithful and wicked servants (Matthew 24:45-51).
- ❖ And finally, the tale of the ten virgins, five wise and five foolish (Matthew 25:1-13).

All three have the same admonition: be prepared! Our Master may return at any moment.

Telling Future Generations

The Old Testament is full of prophecies regarding Jesus'

---

[1] *Lycoris radiata.*
[2] Common names for Lycoris include surprise lily, hurricane lily and spider lily.

incarnation, yet 400 years passed from the time of the last one until His appearance – more than enough time for people to forget or doubt. But God preserved the memory of His covenant promises across all those centuries, as exemplified by Simeon and Anna. Both were devout. Both watched hopefully for the coming of the Savior. Enlightened by the Spirit, they exulted over weeks-old Jesus when He was presented at the Temple, knowing the long-awaited One was before them (Luke 2:22-38).

The wait for Jesus' return is nearing 2,000 years. Unlike the forgotten Lycoris, though, His triumphant arrival is ever on my mind. I rejoice that I am one of those expectantly waiting because generations before me told their children who, in turn, told their children so the marvelous message of God's glorious deeds would not be forgotten (Psalm 78:1-4). Likewise, we must tell our children and grandchildren of His great love and faithfulness and instruct them in His commandments (Deuteronomy 6:4-7).

Called Home

When my mom was a little girl, talk of the impending end of the world scared her. In her wisdom, my grandmother told her, "Honey, the end of the world comes for someone every day." And so it does, sometimes when we least expect it, just like it did for Ray.

Whether we remain until Jesus returns or He calls us Home before, may we be found ready and watchful, faithfully going about our Father's business. Though the timing is unknown, His second coming is as certain as His first, and our eternal destiny is secure.

Come, Lord Jesus!

Acknowledgments

Accomplishing a monumental goal is rarely a solitary task. You need people to come alongside you for the journey, people who will cheer you on to the finish line. I've been blessed to have family and friends who've prayed, encouraged, and provided practical help as I pursued my dream to write this book. If you're one of those people, thank you!

When you're pursuing a dream, it's essential to have folks who believe in you, not only the ones closest to you but also those who are professionals in your field of endeavor. Author Josh Langston was one of the first such people who described my writing abilities as a gift and encouraged me to hone my skills. I've since taken several of his writing classes and have benefitted from his knowledge and patience as he's helped me complete *Be Still*, including designing the cover.

Authors Christina Fox (enCourage[1]) and Sharon Betters (Daily Treasure[2]) also fall into this category. Both have graciously given me opportunities to share my stories with readers of the

---

[1] The enCourage blog (encouage.pcacdm.org) is part of the women's ministry initiative of the Presbyterian Church in America's Committee on Discipleship Ministry.
[2] Daily Treasure is a ministry of MARKINC, www.markinc.org

blogs they oversee. Christina has mentored me throughout the writing process, patiently answering my many questions and pointing me to others who could help, including Elizabeth Turnage. Elizabeth shared specifics on self-publishing her devotionals, details I wouldn't even have thought to ask about.

Author Susan Hunt is my spiritual mother, second only to Mom in that respect. Her ability to identify others' areas of giftedness and nudge them into using them for God's glory has led me to take on challenges I would likely have passed up otherwise.

Even with all this support, I talked a lot about writing a book before I finally got down to the hard work of doing so. When I did, I knew I'd need input along the way and invited several friends to join my Book Advisory Team (BAT). LaVerne Abbott, Ann Beattie, Jean Berwager, Suzanne Boesl, Laurie Chastine, Mary David, Kay Duncan, Jessie Kuipers, Barbaranne Kelly, Denise Monroe, Kelly Stout, and Kathy Wargo kindly accepted the invitation. Over the months since, I've asked them for feedback on everything from cover art to potential titles to formatting, most with the added plea, "please pray for me!" Their prayers and comments have helped mold me and my writing, and their encouragement has kept me going.

As the book began to take shape, I asked Ann, Jean, and Jessie to be my first readers, who would go over the stories searching for typos and grammatical errors. Their own facility with the English language and attention to detail allowed them to catch mistakes I overlooked. (Note: I take full responsibility for any remaining defects since I continued to tweak and tinker with the stories up until moments before turning the manuscript over

Acknowledgements

for formatting!)

Jessie didn't stop at grammar and typos, though. She assumed the role of editor, lovingly put her English degree to work on my behalf, and spent countless hours writing up notes for me. I implemented many of her suggestions and know my stories are more impactful and precise because of them.

And then there's Mom, the most fervent prayer warrior I've ever known. This isn't the first time she's prayed me over the finish line of one of my undertakings. She's been doing so my whole life.

But ultimately, all praise and glory belong to God, for removing my heart of stone, replacing it with a heart of flesh, and enlightening the eyes of my heart to see the hope to which He's called me. In His over-and-above goodness, He's gifted me with the ability to fashion words into stories to convey that hope to others. I pray my efforts will always honor and glorify Him.

www.ingramcontent.com/pod-product-compliance
Lightning Source LLC
Chambersburg PA
CBHW071458080526
44587CB00014B/2141